ATF Series: 8

Church and Civil Society

A Theology of Engagement

Edited by Francis Sullivan and Sue Leppert

The ATF Series is published by the ATF Press. Each volume is a collection of essays focusing on a theological investigation of the interaction between the Christian faith and cultural, social or scientific issues.

ATF Press
Adelaide

The ATF Series
Series Editors
Veronica Brady IBVM and Hilary Regan

ATF Series 1
Faith In The Public Forum, Neil Brown and Robert Gascoigne, editors, 1999.

ATF Series 2
Civilising Community for Us All, Libby Davies and Francis Sullivan, editors, May 2000.

ATF Series 3
More Than a Single Issue: Theological Considerations Concerning the Ordination of Practising Homosexuals, Murray Rae and Graham Redding, editors, 2000.

ATF Series 4
Spirit of Australia: Religion in Citizenship and National Life, Brian Howe and Alan Nichols, editors, 2001.

ATF Series 5
Prophecy and Passion: Essays in Honour of Athol Gill,
David Neville, editor, 2002.

ATF Series 6
Rethinking Religion: Exploratory Investigations,
Douglas Pratt, 2003.

ATF Series 7
Spirit of Australia II: Religion in Citizenship and National Life, Brian Howe and Philip Hughes, editors, 2003.

ATF Series 8
Church and Civil Society: A Theology of Engagement, Francis Sullivan and Sue Leppert, editors, 2004.

ATF Series 9
Faith and Freedom: Christian Ethics in a Pluralist Culture, David Neville and Philip Matthews, editors, 2003.

ATF Series 10
God Down Under: Theology in the Antipodes, Winifred Wing Han Lamb and Ian Barns, editors, 2003.

ATF Series: 8

Church and Civil Society

A Theology of Engagement

Edited by

Francis Sullivan

and

Sue Leppert

ATF Press
Adelaide

First published 2004

National Library of Australia
Cataloguing-in-Publication data

Church and Civil Society: a theology of engagement
Includes index
ISBN 1 920691 19 7

1. Church and the world. I. Leppert, Sue. II. Sullivan, Francis, 1956- III. Australian Theological Forum.
2. (Series: ATF; 8)

261.1

Published by
ATF Press
An imprint of the Australian Theological Forum
PO Box 504
Hindmarsh
SA 5007
ABN 68 314 074 034
www.atfpress.com

Printed by Openbook Print, Adelaide, Australia

Contents

Contents

Acknowledgments

The publishers wish to acknowledge the following organisations and individuals for their kind permission to use their papers in this volume of essays:

- Honourable Alexander Downer's 'Sir Thomas Playford Lecture of 2003'. Copyright Commonwealth of Australia, reproduced by permission

- Scotts Church, a Uniting Church in Adelaide, for the following papers from their 150th Anniversary Series of Lectures, 'Faith in the 21st Century', which were held in July 2001:

    Sir Ronald Wilson's paper, 'Faith and Ethics in Contemporary Sociey'

    Professor James Haire's paper, 'Gospel and Globalisation'

    Honourable Brian Howe's paper, 'Politics and Faith: Living in Truth'

- Australian Catholic Social Justice Council for the paper by Sir William Deane, 'Catholic Social Justice Sunday Statement of 2003'

The publishers also thank the following bodies for their generous financial assistance in the production of this book:

Forum on Faith and Society
Australian Research Theological Foundation Incorporated
Melbourne Anglican Social Responsibilities Committee
Presidents Table, Uniting Church in Australia
Uniting*Care* NSW/ACT
ATF Literary Fund

Introduction

Sue Leppert and Francis Sullivan

Communities have always struggled with how best to care for their members. What is the prudent balance between collective and individual responsibility? Is it possible that we can care too much and not leave room for people to rise to life's challenges and in turn become the fullness of person they have potential to be? Or is this merely a sophisticated justification for permitting a divide between the haves and have nots, between the fortunate and the rest?

These are the questions which go to the heart of being community. They also shape the identity of Christianity. Philosophy aside the discipleship inherent in Christianity involves as much a 'state of the heart' as it does a 'state of the mind'. It can follow that actions may speak louder than words, but words inspire, motivate and lead those actions. The reflected life is worth living!

Therefore the tradition of reflection and discernment of the gospel, the stuff of Christian action, has much to offer a pluralist community seeking better ways to care for all its people. This volume is a collection of such reflections. It not only offers rich insights, it demonstrates the tensions that exist in any healthy dialogue when various impassioned perspectives converge on common ground.

Church and civil society is not a dichotomy. To be church is to civilise the relationships in a community. Human dignity and just treatment of others underpins civil relationships. A society devoid of civility is not a recognisable church community. The challenge is to achieve that quality of relations. It calls for a theology of engagement, not separateness. It demands an intelligent dialogue which enables society to move forward despite the inevitable tensions which arise when some must necessarily be given more because they need more. In short it means finding a practical and explicable way of loving one's neighbour.

This work of theological engagement opens with a minister of the Commonwealth, Tony Abbott, telling us that as a politician, he is more interested in worldly ideals than religious ideals, and more interested in the state of the world than in getting people to heaven. Despite that, Abbott maintains that politicians are 'called' to build a better world, and that call is 'the call to justice, the call to right, the call to good'. Consciously or not, he is echoing some fundamental Christian values, and therefore inadvertently giving us a little foretaste of 'Heaven'.

In engaging church and civil society theologically, we are essentially focusing on that call to justice, to right, and to good. The values of 'church' are not incompatible with the values of 'society'. Indeed, they are fundamental to injecting the 'civil' into civilisation. Senator Chris Evans, a self-confessed 'heathen', welcomes the value, through mission and values, added by the churches and their caring agencies: 'we would rather the church to be a critical and dissenting voice, challenging our values, than to be engaged in a tepid discussion on the price of outputs'.

Alexander Downer believes that many politicians are sincere about their faith, and, echoing Tony Abbott, see their public life as a vocation or 'calling'. Downer also appears more than happy to defend the right of the churches to enter political debates—but there are conditions. Church leaders, he argues, too easily fall into the trap of grandstanding on complex secular issues about which they are ill informed. In addition, they are becoming increasingly sceptical about their faith, and many have moved away from their core beliefs. The church has become involved in the social agenda of the Western world with 'indecent speed', and has neglected to provide consistent moral teaching, and assist Australians to find the 'spark of inspiration' that gives our lives greater moral and spiritual meaning.

This stern criticism is debated with considerable passion in Part II, *Ethical Perspectives.*

Sir Ronald Wilson draws on the prophet Micah's inspiring exhortation to do justice, love mercy, and walk humbly with God. He points to a parallel between the fundamentals of the Christian faith and key moral and ethical challenges of our time: the promotion and protection of human rights, reconciliation, the treatment of asylum seekers, and the ever-growing gap between rich and poor.

In this globalised world, where there is increasingly nowhere to hide, faith and the quality of community life are increasingly exposed to scrutiny. Sir William Deane maintains that the very heart of our national worth and decency is defined by our corporate attitude to others, to who is included or excluded. To discount the opinions and critiques of church leaders who condemn social policy or political decisions as racist or separatist is to discount the relevance of morality in our Australian democracy.

If Christians are to truly pursue justice and peace, and actively demonstrate the relevance of a faith that is willing to take the risk of compassion for the 'other', they must see the way of Jesus as a radically alternative social vision, says Brian Howe. The politics of compassion and interdependence, however, are the antithesis of the increasingly powerful individualism of modern culture, which threatens to obscure the radical meaning of compassion. The church must represent an alternative voice, but can it do so when threatened by the demands of a corporatist and market-driven culture?

Yes! is the resounding encouragement from Allan Patience and James Haire. Firstly, Haire reminds us of how the church gave expression and meaning to the gospel, to evangelism and to mission through various stages in its history. The culture of Christianity has become interwoven with the various cultures of societies and times, and now faces the challenge of both moulding and being moulded by a global world, and potentially, a global culture.

Patience's enthusiasm for embracing the opportunity that comes with globalisation almost leaps from the pages. Mainstream Western Christianity has an incredible opportunity to 'think stirring new thoughts and inspiring new visions', about a re-imagined, re-energised Christianity that is able to play a role in re-shaping globalisation – and therefore advancing the well-being and dignity of all humanity. For an emerging global society to be 'civil', it must become self-aware, developing a profound empathy for the 'other', and offering an inspiring moral and ethical alternative to the prevailing narcissistic, nihilistic 'predatory' globalisation that devalues even further the world's poor and vulnerable. The churches must find a meaningful way to articulate that uniquely Christian ethic of unconditional love, for 'a loveless globalisation is a global nightmare'.

How then, to demonstrate that unconditional love? Part III, *Welfare Perspectives,* reflects on the practical living out of Jesus' radical way – the way of compassion, respect for all, and non-judgemental inclusiveness – and the social and political contexts in which that must occur.

Linda Campbell begins by reminding us that growth and progress go hand in hand with conflict, and that church welfare agencies are no less complex than their non-church counterparts. Employer responsibilities, financial control, accountability and the need to negotiate with a range of stakeholders place considerable demands on church agencies—a challenge to which they rise, perhaps almost too well, developing a stronger symbiosis with the state, than with their parent church.

'Smart politics' has a price, warns Joe Caddy. At risk is not only good policy, but also the moral fibre that is exemplified by openness to all people, respect for the other, solidarity between people, a shared vision for the common good, and priority given to the poor and disadvantaged. Further, the adversarial nature of our political and social systems discourages bipartisan solutions to the 'big questions', and encourage attacks on people who attempt to address the broader issues that may call them to take (or challenge) positions of leadership.

But without the kind of leadership that inspires a shared vision for the common good, how are Christians to stand for truth in the modern world? Hilary Berthon and Lin Hatfield Dodds offer some seeds of hope in the form of policy-based advocacy, planted in the nurturing ground of compassion and social justice, modelled on the life and ministry of Jesus, and aspiring for the ideal of a decent life for all, with a particular tenderness for those who are most disadvantaged.

This thought is taken further by Ray Cleary, who describes the church's mission of compassion as willingness to participate in God's justice (that foretaste of Heaven). He reminds us that the Christian community has always been involved in influencing civil society, but continues to face strong criticism for 'raising the flag' for a more just and compassionate community. 'Feeding the hungry is a noble act, but attacking the cause of hunger is seen as disturbing'. Why is society so threatened about this particular 'call' to justice? Could it be the fear that a revitalised faith will challenge the prevailing social agenda and culture of indulgence?

John Pettman seems to think so, as he points to the contemporary concept of mutual obligation as one of (one-way) coercion and compulsion. It will take more than a legalistic approach to force people to be friendly, generous, helpful, concerned or responsible. It will take a fundamental change of heart and mind—and although the churches and their agencies might be ready for this, and already living it out, why don't governments, corporations, the media and the community at large share this hope for humanity?

Part IV, *Theological Perspectives,* reminds us that as Christians and as church, the responsibility for telling and retelling the story of hope through God's grace is ours. That story must be meaningful and accessible to an ever-changing world if it is to remain life-giving.

Geoff Schirmer gently reminds us that even in the pain and hopelessness of personal and societal trauma, Christ is present with his grace. The Christian's engagement with society is essentially an encounter with Christ, and is therefore shaped by the Christ of compassion. The cross of Christ and the cross of the Christian belong together—so in all that we do, as individual and church, as service provider and advocate for justice, we do because of, through and with the Christ who has been before.

Herein lies a challenge for people of faith. Our Christian faith is founded on 'forgiveness, tempered by judgement', as Harry Herbert puts it. As church, we live out, and campaign for, a more humanitarian society, one where love of neighbour is exemplified through service provision, drawing attention to unmet need, and bringing hope where there is none. With such a profound vision, why is it so hard to engage the corporate heart and mind of Australian society? The churches and their agencies must be politically and socially active, or they risk becoming indistinguishable from private operators, not recognised for the values for which they stand.

And yet for many in our traumatised world, craving for love and hope, the message of Christ is not heard, and the overt messengers, the churches, are seen as irrelevant. Exploring this irony, Stephen Ames acknowledges that there is a 'mismatch' between church and society, a dissonance between what Christ shows to be the truth about the world, and what the world takes to be truth about itself. However, there is also a resonance between the love and compassion only possible through the suffering Christ, and the cries of a suffering humanity only able to be healed and made whole through the touch of divine love. In a world where turbulent social change is now treated as 'natural', only those faith communities that explore faithful and novel ways of engaging our changing social context will bear fruit, and indeed, exist in the future.

Church and Civil Society is a deeply challenging collection of insights. Each author has gone some way toward naming the 'dissonances' that undermine the heart and soul of society, particularly at the level of social change.

How can the churches, and their agencies of care and education, *not* engage, both theologically and practically, in all aspects of society? How can they not recognise that political and social change has deep relevance for spirituality, for mission and for worship, and more importantly, that the reverse is true—that the church's theology and practice, and spiritual expression, are critical to an authentic engagement of faith with this ever-changing world?

The challenge is one of openness to the eternal surprise—the surprise of the divine meeting the human, in spite of the rise, or fall, of 'civilisation'.

Part I

Political Perspectives

Church, Civil Society and Politics

Tony Abbott

I welcome the opportunity to reflect a little on the relationship between the things of God and the things of Caesar, and the relationship between the servants of God and the servants of Caesar.

I think that understanding of these things is constantly evolving in light of practice and one's deeper thoughts and meditations. So I do not offer this as my final opinion on this particular area, but rather as part of the ongoing discussions on these matters which make up this collection of essays.

I spent three years as a student for the priesthood. One of those three years I was doing pastoral work in the western Sydney suburb of Emu Plains—at our Parish of the Lady of the Way. Father Kevin Hannon—my parish priest out there—said it would be good if one Sunday in four I delivered a reflection on the gospel.

I always put a fair amount of work into these reflections—whether I was good at it or not I do not know—but one day I was walking out of church at the end of mass and I overhead two parishioners say:

> 'That guy shouldn't be a priest, he should be a bloody politician.'

Not long after entering politics I was requested by one of my colleagues to speak on his behalf at the opening of a Catholic school. I said what I thought were appropriate things that might inspire people with enthusiasm for their faith. Someone said to me over the subsequent cup of tea:

> 'You should have been a priest, not a bloody politician.'

So you cannot win!

One of the many reasons I decided I could not persist in my studies for the priesthood is that I decided I was really more interested in worldly than religious ideals. I was more interested in the state of the world than trying to get people to heaven. I thought that I had more passionate commitment to my relationships here with my fellow human beings than with Christ—although I believe he is my brother and friend. But in those times and in these times I have never found prayer particularly easy. So that is one of the many reasons I decided I shouldn't persist in priestly studies.

Even so, it is not without a sense of yearning for the higher things. I often find myself feeling a little like I imagine Claudius would have felt in the play Hamlet where he said something like:

> Words fly out. My thoughts remain below. Words without deeds will not to heaven go.

There are tensions between one's ambition for the higher things—one's desire to be a good person in the eyes of God—and the things that one does, as one must, in the world.

I think that politicians are, nonetheless, called to build a better world and that does not just mean increasing GDP and producing better roads and having ever more productive and efficient factories. It also means doing what we can to produce happier families, more caring communities, more courageous citizens who heed the call to justice, the call to right, the call to good.

I think that churchmen and women are called to point us to the next world. To be in the world but not to be entirely of it. But I am certainly not going to posit some sharp dichotomy between the things of the world and the things of the next because faith cannot exist without works.

It is in the realm of good works that the church and the state jostle against one another, and one can either cooperate or compete as the case may be. From the time of Constantine at least the Christian church has been active in the world; producing schools, running universities, building and staffing hospitals, because it is a good thing to educate people, to help people, to have people aspire to the truth. And we give Christian witness by doing all these things well.

In more recent times—in the era since the Renaissance—the state has also striven not just to maintain law and order, not just to protect our borders against external aggressors but—in its own way—to build a happier society. And so the state has also run schools, hospitals, universities and all the other institutions that a sophisticated civilisation believes necessary to try to have happier societies.

I do not believe there is any necessary conflict between the churches's desire to do good works as a way to glorify God and the state's desire to do good works so people can lead happier and more productive lives. I believe there are vast areas in which church and state can—and should—work together.

Anyone familiar with the history of Catholicism in this century would be aware of the long struggle for state aid. In the 1870s and 1880s—right around the country—colonial governments cut out government funding to church schools—and unlike the Presbyterians, the Methodists, the Anglicans and the others—we Catholics decided we were not going to surrender our school system. Our schools were very important to the flourishing of our Catholic faith and, therefore, at extraordinary expense and great personal sacrifice and hardship, we kept the system going for almost one hundred years without any assistance at all.

Not only were we providing Catholic kids with a good education, we were relieving the state of the necessity of providing an education for them. And it was just not fair that our schools didn't receive sustenance from the state. In justice we demanded assistance and finally under Bob Menzies—and subsequently—we began to get it.

The question is not so much the relationship between church and state—because there must be some sort of relationship—but the question is what are the terms of engagement? What can the church expect of the state? What can the state expect of the church?

And when the relationship develops, to what extent is the state subtly seducing the church from its religious mission and when is the church too much infusing the state with values that are really religious values—matters of personal choice rather than civic necessity to be expected of all?

In areas such as school education the state is perfectly entitled to insist on an appropriate academic curriculum as long as it doesn't interfere with such religious formation as a church wishes to provide to its students. In practice I don't think this is necessarily a difficult problem. And if there are times when Catholic schools don't seem that different from state schools I suspect that is because of the conception of Catholicism that the people running them have—not because of any undue interference that the state may have imposed upon them.

As Minister for Employment, I am responsible for employment services provided by the government and in recent years we have replaced the old Commonwealth Employment Service with the Job Network—a range of private, community-based, charitable and religious organisations including the Brotherhood of St Laurence, Centacare, the Salvation Army and Mission Australia—providing employment services which the government pays for but which are delivered in accordance with the particular ethos of that organisation.

These organisations, generally, have been very good at their job. They have been very good at giving people the motivation, confidence, the sense of faith in themselves that is a priceless asset to go out and find a job in a hard marketplace. What's more, there is a certain plausibility in the success that religious Job Network members have had. These days they are highly professional. The idea of a religious Job Network member saying to a few blokes from the St Vincent de Paul 'come along and give a pep talk to job seekers'—if it was ever like that—is long gone. They are highly professional organisations operating according to the best professional standards, but with the additional bonus of not needing to make a profit, nor are they simply relying on professional standards to keep them going.

There is something extra about people with faith in their hearts, and the love of God on their lips, that gives them that extra commitment to job seekers. It's not easy to work with job seekers, particularly the long-term unemployed. Yes, Jesus asked us to love the poor and we try our hardest to do so, but sometimes as human beings it is difficult and I think the religious Job Network members—in common with the others—do a splendid job.

How does the relationship work between church and state in this area? Obviously the state can and must insist on a certain level of service but religious organisations can insist on the freedom to provide the requisite services in their own way. Church organisations can't say whom they will and won't help. That would be quite unconscionable and I don't think any church organisation today would want to go down that path.

It would be wrong for the state to become too prescriptive about, for instance, who church organisations will and will not employ. Some of you might remember a controversy a year or so back when the Human Rights Commission set out draft guidelines for the employment of people in religious organisations delivering government services. Those guidelines, I'm happy to say, have been significantly revised.

But certainly the original guidelines were not about freedom of religion but about freedom from religion. They would have made it almost impossible for church organisations to exist as organisations with a particular religious ethos.

As it happens, I am an imperfectly practising Catholic Christian who is also a politician. But I'm very conscious of the fact that I could never base the policies I pursue as a politician—or I could never expect the policies of the government which I am proud to serve as a Minister—I could never expect them to be based on religious values. Government policies must be based on human values. But I have to say, as a Catholic Christian, there are good human justifications for the positions that my tradition supports.

I think it was Newman who said something like this:

> When religion and science appear to conflict, it is not real religion, it's not real science, or it's not real conflict.

And I have to say that all politicians who understand the nature of society and the way human beings work and the need of all human beings for something transcendent in their lives appreciate the importance of Christianity in Australian culture. Even the most hardened cynic usually accepts that we would be a better and happier country if people took the values of the Sermon on the Mount more seriously. But let me stress, it's people not government, which should do so. There are many things which are the highest virtue in people which would be utter folly in government.

A Christian is called to love. A politician is required to give everyone a fair go. These are quite different concepts but are often confused when Christians give advice to politicians.

Valuing Care: A Heathen Perspective

Chris Evans

I thought it might be easier to debate a mere abbott—rather than the usual bishop—on matters of theology. But the abbott's interest in the issue makes him a formidable opponent.

In thinking about the themes I might explore today I sought the counsel of my father-in-law—a retired Uniting Church minister. He asked two questions:

Firstly, 'Why did they invite you?' He was incredulous that an invitation would be proferred to a heathen. Secondly, he asked, 'How have they defined theology?' I said I thought the steaks were just about done!

I would like to use this address to reflect on what have been profound shifts in the way we deliver care services. I will argue that many of these shifts have served to diminish the value of care. Not because there has been a change in 'who' is providing a service but because of the narrow, economic terms in which the relationship between government and non-government organisations has been couched. I believe that the 'terms of engagement'—as currently drafted—have left us less capable of responding to the diversity of human need and experience.

The challenge for a Labor Government will be to create an environment in which church and community organisations can provide care services in a way that reflects the values of your mission. This will require us to clearly distinguish between the value of caring and its price.

1. Reflections on a changed environment

Non-government organisations have always provided services alongside government. Indeed, in the areas covered by my portfolio—the care of the elderly, children and people with disability—the church has led the development of new and innovative models of care. However, governments now contract for whole programs and have entrusted the delivery of 'core activities' to both the private and not-for-profit sectors.

It is important that we ask what this has meant for both church and state. In what ways has it changed each of us?

Historically, the church has made decisions to provide care and support services in areas where you identified need. Sometimes this was to supplement government services. In education, for example, you have provided places where the study of theology and the provision of pastoral care could sit alongside a secular curriculum.

More often, you have provided services in areas where government has been absent. Decisions have been explicit reflections of your mission.

In recent times, non-government organisations have become a widespread tool of public service delivery. There has been a shift from providing services based on your assessment of need to providing what the government determines it is prepared to pay for.

Current arrangements make it difficult for church agencies to provide care and social support in a way that is consistent with the mission of the church. You are not charged with providing care but with the delivery of a service output.

Narrow output specifications, and compulsory competitive tendering, have assured the pre-eminence of market values in community service contracts. As pressure builds to squeeze more from each taxpayer dollar, it is the values that underpin your mission which are most often squeezed out.

At the same time growing inequality, and changes in work and family life, have increased the demand for the services you are charged with providing.

Clearly these changes present dilemmas, challenges and questions for the church. When the government does not value what you value —when contracts are awarded on the basis of minimum unit costs —there will be tensions between mission and the rather more prosaic commercial realities of running an agency.

I think it is fair to say that many religious and community organisations have accepted both the economic and political rules of the contractual game.

Many of you will say that the availability of government contracts is now a principal determinant of the welfare priorities of the church. That your agencies have been themselves transformed to comply with accountability regimes. That they have become, in effect, 'little fingers of the state'. That your willingness to criticise government in advocating for the disadvantaged is diminished, or at least more measured, if Job Network contracts or bed licences are thought to be at stake.

If changes to the delivery of government services have changed the agent, they have also changed the principal. Government has forgotten why tenders to provide human services should be different from tenders for the provision of pencils or computers.

We have given less recognition to the values which enhance the quality of our services. If the best and brightest at Arthur Andersen cannot write it down or cost it up, then it has no value.

We have engaged with the rhetoric of values but not with their delivery. The contracting out of government services is frequently justified by reference to 'community building' or deference to the 'principle of subsidiarity'. But it is important that we are not seduced by such appealing notions if contractual arrangements strip them of real meaning.

2. **Implications for the state**

The changed environment also raises questions about the proper role of the state in civil society. It is here that Tony Abbott and I diverge. The Minister has stated elsewhere that government cannot create civil society. He acknowledges that government has a vital interest in shared values, but argues that they must be left to others to build and foster. I beg to differ.

When the government makes a decision about what it is prepared to purchase it makes a value judgment.

When it introduces an aged care funding formula that bears no relationship to the cost of providing quality care, it makes a value judgment.

When it makes the provision of aged care contingent on accreditation standards that pay little regard to quality of life, it makes a value judgment.

When it fails to fund time spent attending to the emotional, social and spiritual needs of residents then it endorses a narrow, and wholly medical, model of care. That, too, is a value judgment.

The Howard Government has promoted its 'Social Coalition' in value-laden terms. Terms that are inappropriate to a notion of partnership bereft of meaning, mutuality or trust. The 'Social Coalition' is a mechanism by which the government has withdrawn from the provision of social services, leaving church and charitable organisations to carry the burden of care.

I would argue that when government devolves responsibility for service delivery, it retains responsibility for providing sufficient policy effort and resources to support the delivery of effective programs.

3. Is there a way forward?

It is a relatively straightforward task to identify the tensions and dilemmas in a changed system. It is a more complex and important task to determine if there is a way through.

I think the first thing we must do is cut through the rhetoric. It is difficult to argue against 'partnerships', 'community building' or the 'de-institutionalisation' of people with disability on philosophical grounds. But we need to consider whether these shifts have improved the quality of life of those individuals who require our support and care.

Rigorous and honest analysis provides the ground from which each of us—church and state—can engage with some fundamental questions. If you are prepared to grant a heathen some latitude, I will begin with you.

I think the church needs to ask what it is that you do better. What are the values that you bring to a caring society? And are these values being delivered and reflected in the services that you provide?

In my humble opinion, the church and charitable sector can offer much to the provision of care. You bring a willingness to look at human need in all its dimensions. You bring a preparedness to look beyond the medical conditions and behaviours that define whether an aged care resident is RCS 1 or RCS 7. You are aware of, and attentive to, the spectrum of social, emotional and spiritual support needs of the individuals for whom you care.

This is the theory. What of the practice?

4. **Adding values to aged care?**

I am a frequent visitor to church-run aged care facilities and you clearly run many places which are somehow 'special'. It is something you feel, usually within minutes of arriving. Sometimes this flows from mission. Sometimes from staff—who are there in numbers and committed to their vocation. Or from the empathy and good humour of volunteers. Or from day programs and genial design.

Other facilities appear bereft of mission and are run as lean, commercial operations. I readily acknowledge that much of this is driven by the structure of government funding and the often perverse price signals to which you are forced to respond.

But this is not the whole story. The fact that many of you are able to provide so much more suggests that the provision of quality care is also determined by the choices you make and the values to which you accord priority.

When the not-for-profit sector is considered as a whole, there are some moral questions raised by your choices.

What does it say about your values—and your support for the aged poor—if you accept a smaller proportion of concessional residents than do private providers?

What does it say about your values if you do not take individuals with dementia-related challenging behaviours on cost grounds? Anecdotal evidence suggests that these vulnerable individuals are frequently passed over in favour of less demanding residents. Left to languish on waiting lists, they are eventually picked up by the profiteers—by the few providers who are untroubled by complex care needs, which they neither intend nor aspire to meet.

And what does it say about your values when the Reverend Harry Herbert threatens to pull the Uniting Church out of nursing home care, as Harry does from time to time, on purely commercial grounds?

I will bravely leave these hanging.

I think the other fundamental question for the church is what can you do to ensure that you are able to provide services, which are true to your mission?

In 1999 I was a member of the Senate Committee inquiring into the Government's proposed 'New Tax System'. Many religious and community organisations appeared at the hearings. All opposed plans to reduce the 'fringe benefits tax' (FBT) concessions available to public benevolent institutions. All argued for concessional treatment on the grounds that you provide 'something different'.

Some argued that they catered to minority interests or provided services in those areas where the private sector couldn't make a quid. Others argued that they provided services that were more personal and responsive, enriching what TH Marshall described as the 'concrete substance of civilised life'. For others, values such as social advocacy, choice and diversity justified a non-government welfare sector and the tax concessions that support it. These are all substantial arguments.

I remember asking an association representing not-for-profit hospitals, owned and operated by religious and charitable bodies, what they did that was different. To my naked eye, some of the establishments had more in common with the Hyatt than with public hospitals.

I was more than a bit surprised when the representatives could not cite any examples of difference. They did not claim that they treated different people in a different way or for a different price than did private, for-profit hospitals. Eventually, they took the question on notice.

So I think, in the first instance, the church needs to be clear about, and articulate, what it is that it does differently.

Secondly, I would encourage church-based agencies to vigorously advocate for values.

Let me speak frankly. My meetings with the not-for-profit sector are as squarely focused on the bottom line as my meetings with private providers and their representatives.

The dollars matter because of what they are used to purchase. We need to be debating what this should be. If we are to build public support for a care-centred system, then care must be a reference point in the policy dialogue.

This is not your responsibility alone. In my mind, the role of the state in a civil society includes stimulating, encouraging and engaging in debates about values. Speaking as a member of the Australian Labor Party (ALP), I think we would rather that the church be a critical and dissenting voice, challenging our values, than to be engaged in a tepid discussion on the price of outputs.

5. Conclusion

In conclusion, let me assure you that the Labor Party wants the churches to remain as providers of government services.

From my own perspective, I think it is your dual role as an experienced service provider and an advocate for those who are weak or vulnerable that adds something of value to the systems through which we care.

However, we need to create an environment in which you can bring your values to our systems.

While it may be alright to specify government contracts for pencils or computers in terms of outcomes alone, values other than efficiency are at stake when we are purchasing care of the elderly or the disabled.

We need to ensure that our discourse on care is not bounded by economic concepts and processes. That it is our shared goals as a caring society which direct our economic endeavours.

Sir Thomas Playford Lecture of 2003

Alexander Downer

It is a privilege to be invited to deliver the Sir Thomas Playford Lecture. Much has been written and said about the success, the authority and the honesty of Sir Thomas's political career.[1] But it was also a career that was profoundly influenced by his Baptist upbringing and lifelong commitment to Christian principles. It is from them and the sometimes turbulent relations between church and state that I take my theme today. Let me begin with a personal anecdote.

Listening to the ABC's AM[2] on Saturday morning 19 October 2002 I was dumbfounded to hear the announcer Hamish Robertson say:

> well, the head of the nation's Anglican Church says the Bali Bomb attack was an inevitable consequence of Australia's close alliance with the United States . . . Dr Peter Carnley says terrorists were responding to Australia's outspoken support for the United States and particularly its preparedness to take unilateral action against Iraq.

Here was the head of my own church, reported by the Australian Broadcasting Corporation as rushing to judgment and blaming the Australian Government for bombing incidents in which so many of our people were killed or terribly injured. Whether this report was fair or not, it struck me hard.

There was no concentration on comforting the victims and their families, no binding up of the broken-hearted while a shocked nation mourned. Yet surely that, first and foremost, is what was needed and what we were entitled to expect.

It was a stark reminder of the tendency of some church leaders to ignore their primary pastoral obligations in favour of hogging the

1. Premier of South Australia from 1938 until 1965.
2. 'AM' is a daily morning current affairs program on the government-owned national radio network.

limelight on complex political issues—and in this case a national tragedy—in ways which would have been inconceivable in the Playford era. This is something that has troubled me for some time.

I will always defend the right of the churches to enter the political debates of our time. But they have special responsibilities—to the facts, to their congregations and to their faiths. Too often, it seems to me, the churches seek popular political causes or cheap headlines. And this tends to cut across the central role they have in providing spiritual comfort and moral guidance to the community.

It may surprise some of you to know that an unusually high proportion of federal politicians on all sides are practising Christians who have a sense of faith and listen to what the churches tell us and the rest of the community. Imperfect as we all too obviously are, we're sincere about the faith that nurtured Western civilisation. It is because of our beliefs that we tend to see public life as a vocation—a calling, not just a job. Beyond the theatre of question time, some of the most impressive and heartfelt speeches in parliament arise over questions of conscience where shared values make unexpected allies and cross-party acquaintances develop into lasting friends.

Despite deep differences, Don Dunstan, the young Labor turk and one-time Anglican synodsman, developed a friendship like that with Playford over the years when the premier very often gave him a lift home in his car, on those nights the house was sitting late. Playford was a religious nonconformist. My own denomination is, as I have said, Anglican. These days that means that, like my denomination, I am very often torn between hope in 'the church militant here on earth' and near-despair at her divisions. I remember where once there was a confident global communion, with room for civilised doctrinal disagreement under a canopy of shared belief.

Those days are long gone. In their place, uncertainty or disbelief in the fundamental tenets of Christianity are commonplace among senior clergy. Not since the Enlightenment swept through France has clerical scepticism been so much on the ascendant. I am reminded of the dilemma faced by Louis XVI and his advisers, when the see of Paris fell vacant. In the Gallican church the king had almost as much of a say in senior appointments as in England. The problem was one of finding someone both suitable and orthodox. When, in 1785, the Archbishop of Toulouse was recommended, Louis replied, 'Ah, no; the Archbishop of Paris must at least believe in God'.

The last forty years of the church have seen even core issues of faith such as the resurrrection become the subject of vigorous dispute. Of course it is possible to believe in God in some sense or other without believing in the resurrection, as many good Jewish and Muslim Australians do. But the Christian church has always taught that belief in the resurrection was the central tenet of Christianity. As a politician, I offer no judgment on this issue: just the observation that some church leaders have moved away from their core beliefs. Not surprisingly then, it is often said that we are entering a post-Christian age. Whether there is a terminal decline in Australia remains an open question.

It depends in part on whether you place more reliance on what people say they believe or in their actual church attendance. Forty-three per cent of Australians believe the resurrection was an actual historical event, yet twenty per cent attend church frequently according to the ACS 1998 survey. It may be that the gap can best be explained by what contemporary congregations experience in the pews. Confidence in the church has fallen in recent years—from fifty-six per cent in a comparable survey in 1983 to thirty-nine per cent. Still, the growing role of televised services for an ageing population and the unexpected strength of new Pentecostal, Evangelical and Catholic youth movements may not have been captured in the survey.

However, a post-Christian age poses a relentless question to politicians and everyone concerned with the character of our society. Family life, the education system and the moral instruction provided by other faiths all play an important part. But without consistent moral teaching and example from bodies like the churches, how can most Australians be expected to behave selflessly or consider the common good and abide by any kind of social contract?

Nature can be relied on to some extent through sturdy instincts like parental love. But the ties of kith and kin are less binding; the weaving of the social fabric is less confidently and competently undertaken than in Playford's era. Most of the givens and imperatives in his worldview are now optional—relative rather than absolute. When 'everything is relative' is the best that many clergy have to offer on major moral questions, morality starts to become a matter of convenience, being seen to do the decent thing, what feels good at the time or what you can get away with. This is a kind of ecclesiastical postmodernism.

Those categories may coincide with the good of society as a whole from time to time, but the erosion of a shared sense of the obligations enforced by conscience is disturbing. I should stress immediately that Christian politicians prize their faith primarily because they believe in it, rather than as an instrumentalist might see it as a useful management tool to encourage civic virtue. The lament is not for 'the good old days' in any simple sense, but for foreshortening of a larger notion of what it means to be fully human. Those clergy and theologians who have lost sight of the fundamentals have filled the vacuum with all manner of diversions.

For some, social work has become the be-all and end-all. Environmental causes, feminist and gay agendas and Indigenous rights provide constant grandstanding opportunities. Most intoxicating of all, and most divisive for their congregations, is overtly partisan politicking. Apart from disdain for traditional pastoral duties and pontificating self-regard, how best to explain the clerics who issue press releases at the drop of a hat on issues where the mind of the church itself is unresolved or not yet engaged?

The then Bishop of London, Graham Leonard, put it this way: 'The Church today, having lost her nerve, shows at times an almost pathetic desire to be loved by the world'. Ingratiating oneself with current popular opinion is a doomed strategy. Dean Inge summed it up, saying, 'He who marries the spirit of the age will soon become a widower'. Perhaps that is partly why twenty-nine per cent of Australians feel negative and another thirty-nine per cent neutral or unsure about the church.

As Graham Leonard was wont to remark, bishops and theologians in their public utterance are remarkably vague and uncertain about matters which their faith should teach them with certitude but remarkably certain and dogmatic on matters of considerable complexity and ambiguity about which they have no particular expertise. Hence political and social judgments are delivered with magisterial certainty while utterances on fundamental Christian doctrines are characterised by scepticism and doubt.

I think it is a polite way of saying that if you cannot rely on what they say about what they are supposed to understand, why take all that seriously their opinions on anything else? It is of a piece with the Australian Defence Forces's Anglican bishop, Tom Frame, recently counselling caution about presuming to know the divine mind on strategic questions.

I am not always in agreement with Bishop George Browning of Canberra and Goulburn, but I do agree with his remark that the church had become involved in the social agenda of Western governments with 'indecent speed'. A temperate approach to political engagement would be as welcome now as the end of the Australian Labor Party's attitude to the Catholic Church as a wholly-owned subsidiary.

As Gerard Henderson remarked, the thirty per cent of Catholics on the Howard Government's front bench 'is about the same as the percentage of Catholics in the Australian community'. The old legacy of sectarian bitterness which meant that, as Judith Brett noted, 'Catholics did not join the Liberal Party up until recent times because they felt unwanted', has disintegrated. Unfortunately, the integration of the Catholic Church into the broader body politic as represented in Parliament has not prevented some of its bishops from making intemperate denunciations of Australia's participation in the Coalition of the Willing in Iraq.

The churches, and in particular the Catholic Church, had called for the application of humanitarian intervention in Rwanda, the Balkans and East Timor. They were right to do so—but this contrasts dramatically with the approach of many church leaders to the brutal dictatorship of Saddam Hussein. Few church leaders appeared concerned about the grotesque human rights abuses within Iraq of the Saddam Hussein regime—already the remains of at least 300,000 people have been found in mass graves since the end of the war. Few church leaders expressed concern that Saddam Hussein had used chemical weapons not only against other countries but against his own people. Few church leaders seemed concerned that Saddam Hussein had invaded neighbouring countries at the cost of over one million human lives. Surely that is enough evil to enrage even the most placid church leader.

Instead, vocal church leaders seemed more engaged in an esoteric debate about whether the Coalition of the Willing was adhering to international law—when in fact it was Saddam Hussein who was in breach of that law. To debate international law is fair enough, but these commentators provided a one-sided moral message on war that offered no insight into the moral price the world would pay if it failed to address the vile immorality of the Saddam Hussein regime. These commentators neither confronted that difficult moral dilemma, nor gave clear guidance.

In some cases they apparently failed to understand that for god-fearing people there was a moral dilemma that needed to be confronted. Symptomatic of these types of problems was the retiring address by the President of the Uniting Church, Professor James Haire. He said, '[W]e live in a time of profound turning away from God in much of our social and national life'. He went on to say that he believed

> egged on by both political groupings in the country, we as a nation had reached new depths of political depravity, especially with the duplicity and harshness of the Tampa incident, and the total inability of the Federal Opposition to act as an opposition in the nation, thus depriving this nation of any genuine democratic debate leading up to the election.

I find the accusation of political depravity—not just misguidedness in particular policies, mind you, but depravity—profoundly personally offensive as well as foolish. That he was attacking both the major parties is no comfort.

As I said at the beginning of this speech, Archbishop Carnley, the Anglican Primate, was almost as outspoken and ill-advised on the issue of the Bali Bombings. Not content with his radio performance, he went so far as to issue a press release, compounding the offence. He expressed his 'concern that by targeting two Bali nightclubs in which large numbers of young Australians were known to gather, terrorists were responding to Australia's outspoken support for the United States'.

I felt obliged to respond to this premature and, as later events demonstrated, erroneous posturing and made it clear that we did not know precisely who was responsible for the bombing and the Archbishop needed to be careful before drawing any firm conclusions. Dr Carnley was obliged to 'do a little back-tracking' as they say, especially when the bombers began to speak for themselves about their motives.

We have heard from them mostly that Australians were not deliberately targeted. Rather, the idea was to kill Americans and Westerners generally. One alleged bomber, Imron, declaring, 'Australians, Americans, whatever—they are all white people'. But where one of these terrorists did mention targeting Australia, the motive was a world away from Iraq.

Imam Samudra said Australians were deliberately targeted because 'Australia has taken part in efforts to separate East Timor from Indonesia which was an international conspiracy by followers of the Cross'.

There were other reasons offered, but the ending of the carnage in East Timor and its liberation, one of Australia's most significant foreign affairs achievements and one of which its people are generally and rightly proud, was uppermost in the conspirator's mind.

So Dr Carnley was wrong. And sadly, he was wrong in a way that came dangerously close to suggesting that our foreign policy should somehow be dictated by the actions of terrorists. I firmly believe that when we have to choose between doing the right thing and doing the wrong thing, we should not allow terrorists to influence our judgment.

As Foreign Minister, of course, I am committed to using diplomatic means as all but the last resort in achieving outcomes in the national interest. Diplomacy, once almost the special preserve of the clergy, requires patience, good manners and steadfastness in ascertaining the facts in any particular case—attributes which, among many modern clerics, are in short supply.

There are some signs of hope. In particular, there is the resurgence of youth movements in some of the churches and the thousands of undergraduates who turned out formally to greet Archbishop George Pell when he first visited Sydney University as their new archbishop. The link between the growing, well-documented social conservatism of many young people and religious observance is part of a pattern. Demographically it fleshes out the increasingly plausible hypothesis that the baby boomers'children have tended to skip a generation and prefer the values of their grandparents rather than their parents.

Sir Thomas will be viewing that development with the same optimism that many contemporary politicians feel. The Christian churches, as with other great religions, such as Judaism, Islam, Hinduism and Buddhism, have a central role to play in providing a moral compass to an increasing materialistic world. While many people, although still too few, have material comfort, as they have achieved that state, they have lost much-needed spiritual sustenance.

The greatest challenge today for leaders of all religions is to forgo the opportunity to be amateur commentators on all manner of secular issues on which they inevitably lack expertise, and instead to find the spark of inspiration to give our lives greater moral and spiritual meaning. I know Tom Playford would have wanted them to rise to that challenge.

Part II

Ethical Perspectives

Faith and Ethics in Contemporary Society

Ronald Wilson

'Where do contemporary morals and ethical values come from? Is Christian faith influenced by them or does the faith have an influence on the shape of human endeavour in twenty-first century society?' And I am to look at some of the major influences on faith in society as we begin a new century.

I begin by giving a short answer to part of those questions. I am saying that I believe that contemporary moral and ethical values in Australia are a product of the whole community—from the parliament and the members that make it up through all the community organisations, the non-government organisations and out across to the individuals that make up the Australian community. The term 'civil society', together with the parliament, connote that community. I like the term 'civil society' because it refers to the collective effort of individual citizens expressed either through their individual lives and statements or through the non-government organisations that they join. And of course it includes the contributions of all the faith communities, including those of the Christian faith.

There can be no doubt in my mind that Christian values and discipleship influence the contribution that individual Christians make in their capacity as citizens. Of course, it is widely diffused through the community and will often be invisible, operating in the biblical image of the salt and the leaven, operating like yeast.

The biblical imperatives to an interest in the values that undergird society are quite clear in my view. I state them briefly, going back to the prophets. In the book of Micah, there is the well-known verse that says, 'What does the Lord require of you but to do justly, to love kindness and walk humbly with God'. You cannot really contemplate doing justly and loving mercy, compassion or kindness without relating those values to your daily walk through life.

The New Testament, of course, stands us in good stead with the image of Jesus and his understanding of his own mission as reflected in the fourth chapter of Luke when he speaks in the synagogue of the spirit of the Lord being upon him to let prisoners go free, to clothe the naked and the other things that are mentioned in that verse. I am sure you remember them.

There is also of course the well-known story of the great judgment (Matthew 25), for when the nations of the world were divided into the sheep and the goats, it was the manner in which the nations had dealt with the disadvantaged in their society that determined their destiny.

More evident than the work of individuals, perhaps, is the contribution of the churches to matters of ethics and faith in the community—both in the love of life in their communities and in the nation. I believe the contribution of local congregations in terms of community service is very significant indeed. Their contribution reflects the values of love and compassion issuing in acts of kindness and the active pursuit of social justice for disadvantaged and marginalised sections of the community. It sounds rather ordinary to us, but I think when we come to consider this topic of ethics and faith at work in the community like yeast, you cannot deny the significance of the often unseen but very practical witness in the local community.

Colleen Egan writes for *The Australian* newspaper in matters of faith and ethics, and it was timely that in an article quite recently she expressed the view that there is a noticeable shift in the attitude to church leaders by the secular Australian media and its audience. She mentions the appointment of Dr Peter Hollingworth, the former Anglican Archbishop of Brisbane as Governor-General of the nation; the headlines that greeted Catholic Archbishop George Pell's arrival in Sydney; and the respect accorded to Baptist leader Tim Costello in Melbourne and the Anglican primate, Dr Peter Carnley in Perth. I cite them as examples. Colleen Egan mentions also the enormous respect accorded to Sir William Deane, known as a devoted Catholic layman.

Ruth Powell is mentioned in the same article. She is a researcher for the National Church Life Survey and she is reported as saying that the resurgence of church leaders as political players is coinciding with a growing hunger in the wider community for spirituality and moral leadership. An interesting aspect of the survey tested community confidence in social institutions. You would be glad to know that churches were mentioned, but only fourth in the order behind the police, the health carers and educators. But do not be too despondent, because the churches were well ahead of lawyers and public servants and the banks—that will not surprise you—and the media.

I have no doubt that the Christian and other faiths (you will notice that I consistently associate other faiths with the Christian faith, such is the deep-seated commitment to ecumenism that has been with me for the whole of my life) exercise considerable influence on some very significant movements both on the global scene and in Australia.

Let me look to the global scene first. There is a growing commitment to the promotion and protection of human rights, and this can be related back to the early days following the Second World War when the United Nations was in process of formation. I understand that there was a very strong religious interest at work during those days, with sustained advocacy by a trio consisting of the director of the Churches' Commission on International Affairs together with his Jewish and Islamic colleagues, and that their advocacy was largely responsible for the commitment in the United Nations charter to the reaffirmation of, and I quote, 'the faith of the peoples of the world in fundamental human rights and in the dignity and worth of the human person'. And also they were responsible for the inclusion in the charter of article 68 which required the economic and social council to establish a commission on human rights. Of course, the first major achievement of that commission was the adoption by the General Assembly of the United Nations in December 1948 of the widely acclaimed and influential Universal Declaration of Human Rights.

I like to quote whenever possible the first clause of the preamble to the declaration because it is an inspiring statement and a challenging one as well. I quote: ' . . . recognition of the inherent dignity and inalienable rights of every member of the human family is the foundation of freedom, justice and peace in the world'. The World Council of Churches, at that time only in the process of formation, went on to become and continued to be an active advocate for ecumenism, and for justice and peace on the world scene.

Then there is the World Conference on Religion and Peace that Allen mentioned in his introduction. This is a body of different faiths, religious faiths. It was initiated in Japan in 1970 but it has gained considerable loyalties around the world from different faiths and meets in a world assembly every five years. I have had the privilege of attending one of those assemblies and was most impressed with the way in which it provides a vehicle for the different faiths to work together in the interest of world peace.

On the Australian scene there are a number of issues that are attracting strong commitment for many Australians, including people of faith. In fact, they are faith issues, I believe. The values that underlie and energise them are closely aligned with both the Christian faith and the faiths of other religions.

The first one I mention is the issue of eradicating world poverty and underdevelopment. I have had the privilege for the last four years of being the president of the Australian Council for Overseas Aid. And it is surprising. I came to it from seven-and-a-half years with the Human Rights and Equal Opportunity Commission and it was interesting that I found it to be just as inspiring and worthwhile as my earlier efforts.

Community education on overseas aid and its importance is focused on the eradication of poverty worldwide. Poverty is a dreadful scourge in the human family which sees, at the present time, something like 1.2 billion—almost twenty per cent of the total population of the world—that is living on the equivalent of one dollar (US) per day. The eradication of at least some of this level of poverty seems to be aided by promoting sustainable development in developing countries where most of them live. There is a strong conviction that sustainable development is best achieved in a country which respects the democratic process, practises transparency in public life and promotes protection of human rights for all. I find that these objectives and these commitments are very close to matters of faith and in fact require the exhibition of faith to promote them.

The second issue I mention is the process of reconciliation. It has been my privilege to be identified with that process through the entire decade of the nineties. And if I might just recall how it began, I believe it is instructive as to what that process is all about.

It began with the inquiry of the Royal Commission into Aboriginal deaths in custody. A commission which roamed widely around the country and engaged in an enormous amount of work over the four years to try to understand what it was that drove Aborigines to constitute such a high percentage of prisoners in custody and which so often led to them taking their own lives. What exactly put them in such a predicament? The inquiry to find the answer went back into the lives of those people in the communities where they grew up, into the cities where they lived in relevant cases, and examined in depth the social relationships between Indigenous and other Australians. There were

339 recommendations to that inquiry. And the 339th was perhaps the most far-reaching of all. It said, in effect, that, if ever the personal discord, injustice and division that characterises Australian life is to be overcome, there must be a concerted effort by all leaders—political and community leaders—in the urgent promotion of a process of reconciliation. That report was published in May of 1991, and it is wonderful to look back and see that in less than four months that recommendation had been acted upon to such a good effect that the Australian parliament enacted the Council for Aboriginal Reconciliation Act unanimously. Despite the spread of parties and independents and so on that make up the national parliament, every member of the parliament present in the house on that day (I cannot speak for absentees, I do not know if there were any) voted for that act. It had some inspiring clauses in a preamble which (and here I am relying on my memory) acknowledged, firstly, the fact that Aboriginal people had occupied Australia for many thousands of years and, secondly, that they had been dispossessed of their lands without consultation or compensation, and thirdly, that there had never been any attempt at reconciliation of the divisions arising from those wrongs. And fourthly, that it was timely that there be such a reconciliation before Australia comes to celebrate its centenary.

And so the council was established. With only a nine-year life, it met first in December 1991 and it went out of existence in December 2000 pursuant to the belief expressed in the preamble, that it was to be a concerted process focused on a specific term, nine years to the centenary. In many ways it was a terrific decade because there was enormous apathy that had to be overcome. I had the privilege of being a member of the first council, whose first term was three years. I spent a lot of time in those three years going around talking to communities and church groups and other groups in the community about the process and seeking to counter the apathy of many of those meetings. And on the part of the Indigenous people wrestling with understanding the use of the term *reconciliation* because the strict dictionary meaning of reconciliation is to *re-establish* a relationship. And try as they might, many Aboriginal people found difficulty in tracing back to any relationship that had been broken. There had never been a relationship to start with in the experience of many Aboriginal Australians.

We had these difficulties to begin with. But recall the events of the year 2000. Wasn't it a fantastic year! It was wonderful to see the corroboree of 2000 when so many political leaders—all the premiers, the prime minister, the leader of the opposition—gathered, while the governor-general was standing on the stage in the opera house and receiving from children representing the future of the united nation, and handing out the documents of reconciliation that had been prepared by the council after enormous consultation throughout the length and breadth of the land.

There were two documents: a Declaration for Reconciliation, setting out the aspirations that underlay the reconciliation process—that were guiding it to fulfillment; and then associated with it, a 'Road Map' providing details as to how that reconciliation goal might be achieved.

The next day after that moving ceremony in the opera house, there was that extraordinary walk across the Sydney Harbour Bridge. I happened to be staying in the hotel just next to the North Sydney railway station and from 6:00 in the morning I could hear this din outside. I looked out the window and there were hundreds of people gathering with the intention of walking down and over the bridge, starting at 8:00 am. It is estimated that there were something like 300 to 350 thousand Australians who walked down onto the bridge, across the bridge and into Darling Harbour, where there were songs and concerts celebrating the occasion that lasted through the afternoon. But it was fantastic to be a part of that walk. It was a good coverage, a good cross-section of Australians —Indigenous, non-Indigenous, elderly people in wheelchairs being pushed, children in prams, family groups and a terrific spirit.

And there was a plane—a small single-engine plane—completely unrehearsed and unplanned, which on the initiative of the pilot, chose to go and skywrite alongside the bridge as the people walked. The word he wrote was 'Sorry'. There was quite a strong wind blowing so he did three 'sorrys' altogether and so at the end you had 'sorry' being pushed towards the harbour heads, then nearer the bridge another 'sorry', and then a third one nearer the bridge again.

There was a lovely story about a woman who lived up-country in New South Wales. She was invited to the walk by the National Sorry Day committee which operates from Canberra, and she said, 'No way, I am too bitter, I will not have a bar of that walk'. But eventually she was prevailed on to come, still expressing bitterness and grief and frustration over the way, the unfair way, she had suffered. But she reported afterwards that gradually as she walked in this crowd, that sense of bitterness began to recede but it was when the word 'sorry' appeared in the sky that it struck her heart and lifted the veil of hurt and trouble that she had received. She was of course a member of the stolen generations, and that 'sorry' reached her heart and began the healing process that she needed so badly. It is a lovely story.

And that is just a brief indication of the importance of the prime minister making an apology in the parliament where there would be no possibility of legal consequences coming from an apology expressing the mind of the nation's parliament, because what is said in parliament is absolutely privileged from reliance in any court proceeding. We recommended an apology after the national 'Inquiry into the Stolen Generations' because of the way so often—time and again—the story-tellers would end their courageous sharing of their story. I say 'courageous' advisedly, because time and again I would sit down at a table, and turn on a tape with the story-teller sitting opposite me, the door would be closed and nothing would happen. Silence. And after ten seconds or more I would look at the face of the story-teller and I would see the muscles working that face to try to stem the tears that were welling in the eyes. It was not until those tears had broken free and coursed down the story-teller's face that the words would come. It was an extraordinary experience. It changed my life to sit there—a representative of the race that had forcibly removed children from the most sacred relationship in a young person's life, the association and dependence on his or her mother. These stories would come with enormous difficulty. You could virtually see them being wrenched out of the heart. It was a hard moment, and I could only sit there and respond to it by opening my heart to those stories. And leave with a deep sense of trust.

We heard 535 personal stories altogether and we had access to another 1500 in writing. But it imposed on me a very deep sense of trust to help all Australian learn something of these stories and the experiences that were still being felt by a significant section of the Australian community in the late 1990s.

It is not ancient history. The latest incident of removal was a dramatic one. There may have been others. The one we heard about concerned a forced removal without the consent of the parents. I am not talking about children who were made wards of the state because of neglect, or anything like that. But the most recent incident that we heard of was as recently as 1971 when a two-year-old boy was taken from Darwin, brought down to Perth and put up for adoption as a ward of the state. No consent from his Aboriginal father and Aboriginal mother. This was not a case of mixed-descent children. This was the child of two full-blood Aboriginal people. Anyway, to be adopted in Western Australian at that time you had to have the assent of a Supreme Court judge. Somehow the parents gained legal aid to appear, a lawyer appeared for them in the Supreme Court and the case went for five days. At the end of the five days, the judge had really reached the end of his patience, and he said,

> I feel this has been a dreadful way to spend time these five days. This child's place is with his parents and if I had the power to order his immediate return to the custody of his parents I would do it. Unfortunately my only jurisdiction is to grant or refuse the order for adoption. And I refuse it.

And so the lawyers went off to the director of the department, the Child, Family and Children's Services Department, told them what the judge had said, and asked, 'Please can we have the child released to the parents?' 'Not on your life!' was the response. In effect he is a ward of the state and he will remain a ward of the state. So the parents went to the minister and the minister was even more emphatic that the child would not be released.

It is difficult to comprehend that this is what forced removal meant, as recently as 1971. We heard these stories, and time and again as the story-tellers got up to go, tear-stained faces and all, they would say, 'I feel better'. And it demonstrated to us the therapy of story-telling. It is a wonderful gift I believe for a community to encourage the telling of stories, because it promotes community. If you have a story-teller and a sympathetic listener, it promotes healing and it is very good for community.

But they also said, 'I would love to know why they did it and that they are sorry'. And so in the forefront of our recommendations—the 54 recommendations that we made—we recommended that the state parliaments that had passed the laws under which forced removals took place in the states, and the national parliament that passed laws or had the legislative power over the Northern Territory, should express apologies for the suffering that had been caused by these misguided policies earlier this century. There has been a lot of misunderstanding in the debate over whether the prime minister should apologise to the stolen generations or not.

An apology is not an admission of responsibility for the wrong that was done—of personal responsibility or even governmental responsibility (although that is a little closer to the bone if you are the successor of the government, if you are the government that actually perpetrated the policies in the first place). But to understand what is meant by saying sorry, it is easier to focus perhaps on when you go to a funeral, or when you meet up with someone that is suffering a personal loss, and you share your sorrow with them. You say, 'Look, I am so sorry for what has happened to you'. It is not an admission that you are responsible for what has happened to cause the grief. It is a very human trait desiring to demonstrate solidarity with the person who is suffering. That is what the stolen generations in this day and age still need—some show of solidarity on the part of the government and the national parliament representing the whole community with the continued suffering of this important section of it.

The Journey of Healing is an important part of reconciliation process and on 26 May every year there are hundreds of occasions where Australians meet together—Indigenous and non-Indigenous —reflecting the journey of healing of the stolen generations. The 26th of May is the date on which the report, 'Bringing Them Home', was tabled in the national parliament. The first anniversary was described as 'Sorry Day'. There were over a million Australians that signed their names into sorry books on that day. They were delivered to Indigenous representatives as expressing the mind of the nation and the 'sorry'. Since then it is described as the anniversary of 'Sorry Day'. Every 26 May is a time for telling stories and for furthering the process of reconciliation, expressed in the growing understanding that will bind Indigenous Australians with other Australian.

Friends, to me this is faith business because the values that underlie it are those basic human values that make us one. The unity of the entire human family that stirs up those feelings of love and affection and commitment to one another are very close to our experience of the faith.

I have spoken of the journey of healing, and then there is Australia's treatment of asylum seekers. This is a faith issue that prompts the growing anxiety of many Australians throughout this land for the seemingly harsh treatment of our asylum seekers arriving on Australia's shores. They are only a trickle really, 4000 is the highest reached in any one period of twelve months. Four thousand people arriving, seeking asylum. Some people have dismissed them quite coldly as well-heeled people who have plenty of money and have arrived in this country. I think partly it is because of the way in which the issue has been presented. I work with these people. In a punitive approach by the government, they are provided with only temporary protection visas. The government accepts that they are genuine refugees but when they first arrive they are put in detention and they stay there whilst they are checked out. In many cases they have lost their papers to the people-smugglers to whom they turned in their desperation to find a new future in a country like Australia. But nevertheless, they give details and the Australian government checks back through the countries from which they have come to establish their status.

Over ninety per cent of them are established as genuine refugees. That is to say, they are human beings who are fleeing from persecution and in whom the international human rights law vests a right to asylum. It is quite wrong to refer to these people as 'illegals', as the media does so regularly. They are not 'illegals'. At worst they are 'unauthorised arrivals' but vested with an international human right to seek asylum from the persecution from which they are fleeing.

This is a faith issue, and I am glad to say increasingly the churches are taking up the concerns on their behalf. They are making their protests for the inhumane treatment of these people. They are genuine refugees and under international law they are entitled to a permanent visa to stay in this country. Oh, no. Not for these people. Genuine refugees although they may be, they are granted only a protection, a limited protection visa—what is called a temporary protection visa. It lasts only for three years and if they are to stay beyond that time, they must again prove their status as refugees. To do that they have to re-establish the genuine fear of persecution and demonstrate that it is continuing, as of now, when this is happening after the three years of their status as refugees.

During that three-year period when they have a temporary visa they are not allowed to seek family reunions; they cannot bring their families to join them in Australian; they are not allowed to access the government-funded English classes (which seems quite stupid really because the quicker they can learn English the quicker they can become productive people in Australia). That is the punishment to be accorded to them. They cannot access the English classes that are provided to other refugees. And they cannot access a number of the government welfare services that are available.

So the churches have stepped in, sought volunteers, and in Western Australia with which I am more familiar (but I understand it is happening in the other cities), volunteers are welcoming them to 'welcome houses' and teaching them English, trying to help them with accommodation, to sort out the written forms that they must complete. To complete these without a knowledge of English is not easy; to access Medicare and achieve access to some other allowances that are available to them is a very hard road that the asylum seekers are committed to at the present time.

I go every Tuesday afternoon to try to teach English to asylum seekers. I am quite convinced that I was never cut out to be an English teacher, but we have a lot of fun. They are mostly young men —Afghans from Afghanistan and Iraq—and despite what they have been through, their smiles are quite ready and there is a healing process that goes on through those volunteers.

As I say, I believe there is an underlying faith that commits—that impels—this kind of recognition of human need and the longing to serve the people in the way that Jesus set forth and in his words.

Finally the faith issue that I want to leave you with in the modern world is the growing gap between rich and poor in Australia. I know you can rattle statistics around and they do not convey a lot, but the most recent statistic I have seen affirms, through the Australian Bureau of Statistics, that 600,000 children (and it has been estimated at 800,000 so this is a lower estimate, though I doubt if it reflects an improvement in the situation) are living under the poverty line—that is, the line that has been established following the Henderson Inquiry into Poverty which has been accepted as the line below which people really have to struggle with poverty to have a decent life.

Another estimate has put the number of children living with a single parent in poverty at something between 600,000 and a million.

On the other hand, we have these gross displays of wealth. I suggest to you this is a faith issue too, for the churches. In a sense the churches have first-hand experience because of their mission work in the cities, because of their first-hand experience of people who, despite their deep sense of dignity, are forced to come seeking handouts. In many cases it is contrary to every bone in their body to be in that kind of position, but their family circumstances or the children for whom they are responsible, are such that they nevertheless do it. The churches do a great work alleviating that poverty and making known, as they have been doing recently, just how desperate the situation is, with the increasing numbers of people seeking this kind of help, and the limited resources available.

I have sought to mention some of the faith issues as I see them in Australian life today, and I could go on with things like mandatory punishment, which is such an evil system in its consequences—in its discrimination against Aboriginal people because they are the people who are the poorest, very often the homeless and very often the most likely to commit the simple property offences such as stealing a bottle of milk from the refrigerator. It is these kind of petty property offences that most likely attract the mandatory sentences to imprisonment which are totally out of character with the seriousness of the crime committed.

Finally I want to conclude by reminding you that we live in a globalised world, a world where there is nowhere to hide. The faith, the different faiths and the quality of community life of every country may find itself, and I believe does find itself, increasingly exposed to scrutiny in a global marketplace of ideas. Such scrutiny I believe does influence the shape and content of faith in society.

But I like to think that globalisation is bringing closer the biblical image of the unity of all humankind.

Catholic Social Justice Sunday Statement of 2003

William Deane

The Australian Catholic Social Justice Council was established by the Australian Catholic Bishops' Conference in 1987 as the national justice and peace agency of the Catholic Church in this country. That being so, the statement which is being launched this year—*A Generous Heart in the Love of Christ: Challenging Racism in Australia Today*—is of obvious importance to Australia's Catholic community. It is also of significance to our nation as a whole. One reason why that is so is its subject matter, namely, our attitude to racism and the importance of the inclusion, rather than the exclusion, of those who are particularly vulnerable through racial, religious or cultural difference. That subject matter lies at the heart of our national worth and decency in these difficult times. Another reason for the statement's general importance is that it represents not only a statement of Catholic principle but also an exposition of the basic standards and values accepted by all Christians, regardless of particular denomination.

One cannot, of course, fail to be conscious of the fact that these days there seems to be a tendency to criticise the leaders of our Christian churches for presuming to speak out on politically controversial matters such as our nation's treatment of asylum seekers and the claims of the disadvantaged, including our Indigenous peoples. With due respect, any such criticism is misconceived. It wrongly discounts the relevance of morality in our Australian democracy. It ignores the importance of the mission of both the Catholic and universal Christian church in a community such as ours where more than a quarter of the population acknowledge their Catholicism and where more than two thirds of the population assert their adherence to one of the Christian denominations. It reflects a failure to understand the essential nature and function of the Christian church and its mission in the modern world. In the discharge of that mission, our church leaders are entitled to be heard in relation to matters, however politically controversial, in respect of which Christian principles and beliefs might provide relevant guidance. They have a clear obligation to themselves, to their calling, to their communities and to our nation, to ensure that their views are known and understood.

For at the very heart of the mission of the contemporary Christianity there lies the obligation to respect, to assist and to speak out for the most disadvantaged and vulnerable members of our society. Indeed, as St Matthew (chapter 25) unambiguously tells us, the ultimate assessment of the life of each us depends, according to the Christian message and ethos, upon how we have treated—and seen Christ in— the most vulnerable and disadvantaged of our fellows . . . those in need of food, drink and clothes; the sick; the imprisoned; and, perhaps most relevant for present purposes, the homeless. And the parable of the good Samaritan makes plain the uncomfortable truth that, for the purposes of that assessment, we cannot confine our fellow human beings to those who share our religion, our race, our culture or our nationality.

The statement we are launching recognises that those basic moral truths constitute an essential message of Christianity in our modern world. It is that message which defines and informs a generous heart in the love of Christ

There are two aspects of the statement to which I would make specific reference. One is it powerful rejection of racism and religious bigotry—of exclusion or discrimination by reason of racial, ethnic or religious difference. In that and in its frank and honest acknowledgment of past injustices in our land, the statement seems to me to provide convincing moral support for the mutual respect and acceptance which lie at the heart of our Australian multiculturalism. That moral support comes at a most appropriate time since, as the statement points out, that mutual respect and acceptance are currently being subjected to extraordinary pressures in our community.

My years as governor-general taught me many things, Perhaps the most important of them all was how critical our multiculturalism is to the wellbeing of our nation. One sometimes hears suggestions that multiculturalism is divisive. I respectfully disagree. For me, multiculturalism *means* inclusiveness, not division. It has enabled us to blend the many into a pretty harmonious whole without bringing to this land old hatreds, old prejudices and old conflicts. It is our multiculturalism in that sense which inspires and sustains our modern Australia. It is not only a moral imperative. In the context of our history and identity, it is also a pragmatic necessity.

The second aspet of the statement to which I would make specific reference is related to the first. It is the recognition of the perhaps inconvenient effect of the Christian message of charity and inclusion in so far as the treatment of refugees or asylum seekers is concerned. At least those of us who are Catholics cannot simply ignore what the Holy Father has recently described as the 'the Christian duty to welcome whoever comes knocking out of need'.[1] Some years earlier, as the statement reminds us, the Holy Father[2] had applied the words of St John to the case of the foreigner who comes seeking help: 'If anyone has the world's goods and see his brothers and sisters in need, yet closes his heart against them, how does God's love abide in him?'[3]

Sometimes, of course, that Christian message can be almost impossibly hard. Certainly, perfection in its implementation is beyond the attainment of almost all, if not all, of us. There are, however, some minimum standards of Christian generosity and charity which are within the reach of all of us as individuals and, collectively, as a nation. It is those minimum standards, rather than any impossible quest for perfection or any unqualified denial of the need for some basic controls or safeguards, which constitute the solid basis of a critical point which the statement seems to me to make. For, as I read its measured language, its seems to me to compel the conclusion that, by *any* acceptable measure of Christian morality, we Australians are losing our way in so far as our treatment of refugees and asylum seekers is concerned.

I quote the words of the statement:

> In Australia, the desire to exclude is expressed most clearly in a hostile attitude to refugees and asylum seekers. The refusal to allow the asylum seekers on the Tampa to land, the excision of parts of Australia so that those are now places where people cannot claim refugee status, and the detention for prolonged periods of people, including children, behind barbed wire fences in the most inhospitable parts of Australia are powerful symbols of Australian exclusion. Those

---

1. Message for the 89th World Day of Migration and Refugees (2003).
2. Message for World Migration Day 2000.
3. 1 John 3:17.

> policies . . . have won the support of a politically significant number of Australians, many of whom themselves were once welcomed as refugees.

I venture the thought that the fact that a politically significant number, or even a majority, of Australians might genuinely disagree, serves only to increase the need for the voice of Christian principle to be raised and heard.

I sincerely congratulate all associated with the preparation of the statement. It is an outstanding and timely document.

I commend the Catholic Social Justice Statement for 2003, *A Generous Heart in the Love of Christ: Challenging Racism in Australia Today,* to my fellow Australian Catholics.

I would add that I particularly commend the statement to our young Australian Catholics. I sincerely hope that it will help them to accept that life does have greater meaning than material success and possessions and to understand that the Christian church's mission of care and compassion for the most vulnerable and disadvantaged of our fellow human beings also provides the ultimate test of our worth as individuals and as a nation.

Politics and Faith: Living in Truth

Brian Howe

I have been asked to comment on the dilemmas faced by a person of faith in politics. What does it mean to 'live in truth'? In seeking to answer this question I would refer to my own journey in matters of faith, then comment on the churches' impact on society and conclude by referring to a possible policy agenda which you might find both interesting and challenging.

There has been a long struggle, I think, especially in Protestant circles, to escape from the pietist view which is that faith is essentially an internal and private matter, not in any direct way influencing the way we live our lives in the community, let alone politics and public life. That is not my belief, that is not my experience. As Rufus Black has pointed out, 'while prayer may be a private matter, beliefs in God and right and wrong are not'.

I would emphasise the personal because of the close link between our faith and risk. Faith represents something of a venture, a journey, a risking of oneself. This does imply making choices and decisions in which the outcomes are often not clear. This sense of risk links closely with the meaning of Christian discipleship.

Rufus Black understands the tension between the personal and the public. He says:

> being public about what is personal is difficult for the very reason that you are making something of yourself public property. Even with a reasonable degree of ego strength it is impossible not to feel the pain and joys, criticisms and affirmations. Some of the charges certainly assail the self. If you engage with the bold claims that are sometimes required to attract attention, there will be mutterings about arrogance. But if you voice the doubts and uncertainties that are an integral part of the humility and plausibility of religious belief, the charge of undermining faith writ through as it is

with condescension for the majority, is sure to follow. (Black 2001, 10)

Faith is a shared faith within the church, the community that is **for us** as Christians our primary community where we are nurtured in our faith. However, we do not live in the church but in the various communities and networks that make up our lives. It is within these broader communities and networks that our faith is being worked out in the way that we live our lives and in the choices we make with respect to all the dimensions of human and created existence.

In the 1950s and 1960s when I was studying theology great emphasis was placed on the presence of God within history—'the God who acts'—the revelation of God in Jesus Christ as an expression of God's presence in history. Christianity was seen very much as a historical religion, which could not be understood or appropriated without coming to terms with the biblical record. This record of faith was read within the church and participated in through the liturgy and sacraments. This context was very important. One felt oneself constantly evaluating the biblical narratives and their interpretation against the background of what the church has been and what the church represented in the world today. As in a family young people constantly question the deed against the word and decision, so it is within the church .The community of faith is also a community of doubt and constant re-examination, yet it is called to witness to and participate in God's action in the world.

During the 1960s there was something of a revolt within the church and among theological students. This was a period in which younger people were questioning traditional authority and seeking to play a *more positive* role in making their own futures. Many theological students felt that in modern Western secular technological society the cultural differences between the ancient biblical world and modern society were so great that *the impact* of the biblical stories and teachings *was being lost*. Sociologists such as Peter Berger in his *Noise of Solemn Assembles* (1961) complained that Christianity in practice was losing its edge and becoming far too accommodating to the values of the white Anglo-Saxon Protestant middle class. Bishop Spong has been echoing many of these concerns that were expressed so strongly in the sixties in his most recent book, *Here I Stand* (2000). Spong in terms not dissimilar to those of Bishop John Robinson in *Honest to God* (1963), *The New Reformation* (1965), argues that much of Christian belief is buried in first century mythologies of little relevance to contemporary life. Indeed, by presenting myths as fact people were being encouraged to deny obvious facts. Like Berger, he is most concerned about the complacency which cultural religion fosters.

> For most people, religion doesn't serve the function of searching for the truth. It is about making people feel secure. If you're a Protestant and you accept that the bible is the unerring word of God or if you're a Catholic and you believe the pope is infallible you don't have to think. You just accept the authority of the church. (*The Age* , 21 June, *In Search of the New Christian Reformation,* Spong 2001)

There is no doubt that many Christians (along with many in other religions) are fundamentalists, as Spong suggests, but the problem with fundamentalists is not so much their complacency as their tunnel vision and sometimes their fanaticism. Undoubtedly many people who belong to the church want to have a private and comforting religion, not one which involves commitment and risk. Increasingly this essentially conservative view seemed to reflect a cultural religion remote from the biblical record. I think, whether the tendency is fundamentalism or pietism, there is the sense that God is present in our past and or within us, not present in our future. I think I took from the Bible and from the preaching and teaching of the church a recognition of the reality of evil but also the possibility of reconciliation. My experience of the church then was that it was struggling to articulate and live out a message of hope and reconciliation in the face of the nuclear threat and in the 1960s in the struggle against racism and poverty and oppressive post-colonial wars such as the Vietnam war. I was impressed with those who were living out their faith and personal commitment in the world. I was also impressed by their capacity to defend their position in ways which were persuasive and in ways which changed things, not just in a political sense, but in ways which changed the culture. Martin Luther King is an example from this period. Desmond Tutu is a more contemporary example.

This dual challenge to people to seek justice and peace is so central to our mission and at the same time so dependent on the way that people understand themselves and the nature of their faith. The words of the prophets continue to inspire our literature and our culture, but our central message still focuses on the person Jesus. This is so because for Christians this person embodies that which has inspired so many to put their bodies on the line for their faith It is his capacity to speak in terms which become contemporary that is so central to the miracle of faith. That is why it is so important to return to the biblical story and re-examine its meaning in terms which make sense in this generation.

In the 1960s I thought sociology was most useful in understanding issues of church and society. More recently I have been impressed with the way that sociological tools have helped us to get a much better understanding of who Jesus was, how radical was his message and yet to me so contemporary in its implications and its force. This is reflected in part in the writings of the New Testament scholar Marcus Borg, who sees the struggle to articulate an alternative wisdom as central to the life and teaching of Jesus. In a sense, at the heart of his political struggle against the temple was his commitment to an alternative wisdom which emphasised the spirit of God as being a spirit of compassion which implied an end to the distinctions which were reflected in the power structure of the Palestine in his day and which Borg describes as a self-serving purity system. The system was self-serving in that the benefits of the system flowed through to those who controlled the temple. The result of this system had been to create a world with sharp boundaries; between pure and impure, righteous and sinner, whole and not whole, male and female, rich and poor, Jew and Gentile. 'But in a society ordered by the purity system, the inclusiveness of the Jesus movement embodies a radically alternative social vision' (Borg, 1994, p 56). 'In Christ there is neither Jew nor Gentile, slave nor free, male nor female.' The politics that Jesus preaches and teaches is a politics of compassion and interdependence, the antithesis of the increasingly powerful individualism characteristic of modern culture. This individualism, Borg argues, obscures the meaning of compassion (Borg, 1994, p 60). In similar terms many would argue that an unchecked free market system works to concentrate wealth and power and destroy the basis of cooperation and public or communal values. Same theme, different temples.

Christians are people so moved by witness of the biblical accounts of this person Jesus that they seek to join his struggle to make justice and compassion the central theme of our lives and a reality in the world in which we live. Their ministry in the world is work to remove those barriers which prevent people from realising their inheritance in Jesus Christ, that is, the capability to become more fully human.

Having mentioned Borg and his interpretation of what was happening in first century Palestine, I want to go on to answer the second question that has been posed to me. That is, how does faith find expression in this major influence on the shape of society'?

I began by stressing the importance of church itself, 'God's Colony in Man's World' (Webber, 1960) or without the sexist connotation, 'the resident aliens'. In the thought of the theologian Stanley Hauerwas the church exercises influence in society most of all by just being the church—by demonstrating in its life the compassion of God as reflected in the life and teachings of Jesus. He is an anticipation of the kingdom. God's rule is characterised by mercy. His kingdom is not one marked by coercion, but his demands on those who follow him are uncompromising. His cross is not so much a symbol of self-sacrifice as a sign of God's present rule. God's people live by way of God's forgiveness and make possible the fellowship, which is a defining mark of the church. Hauerwas has a communitarian vision in which he represents the church as an alternative polis, an alternative form of politics. What the church should be about is 'living in truth', demonstrating the integrity of the gospel in word and deed.

The church, he argues, is a community of virtue whose task is not to remake the world but to be patient and never lose hope. The church should feel called to be faithful, not effective.

Hauerwas is concerned that Christians, churches, in the desperate desire to win acceptance, will loose the tension between the church and society. There is the danger that words important in the biblical tradition and church traditions will be separated from those traditions and will be appropriated and used in ways which are no longer challenging. Principles will be advocated which are devoid of content. Certainly it is important that the church is itself 'living in truth', that is, that it continues to be committed to the poor and the disadvantaged and is seen to be the servant church of the servant Lord. However, in an era of corporatism and massive advertising budgets, it is becoming increasingly difficult to read the actions of the church and to sort the wheat from the chaff.

The Australian newspaper's dossier on the Salvation Army comments on its carefully cultivated image of a compassionate social service organisation 'But God's work has also become very big business. If the Salvation Army were a company it would sit comfortably in Australia's top 200. It holds net assets of at least one billion dollars and has a healthy annual income nestling at about $350 million' (*The Australian* 23–24 June 2001). It is not only the Salvation Army which has adopted the methods of large corporations and seek to compete aggressively in the marketplace for large corporate contracts. The agencies of a number of other churches and religious groupings have adopted similar strategies and made corporate or financial success a very important if not the most important measure of their success. This is not to say that the Salvation Army or other church-based welfare agencies do not provide efficiently and effectively important social services. It is rather the freedom of the church to be the church which is threatened by its accommodation to the demands of a corporatist and market-oriented culture. What room is left for the church to represent an alternative voice? Where is the necessary tension as between church and society? As Brian Watters recognises, the Salvation Army, despite its incredible success, is on a knife-edge: 'My feeling is I don't know whether I'm seeing the death throes of the Salvation Army or its rebirth.'

Faith communities can influence society by presenting an alternative polis through building communities which by their mode of being have an influence on society. The churches can have influence in the way that they provide services and reach out to serve the community. However, churches are also important because of their freedom to represent an independent view from the state. John Bannon in an address to the Spirit of Australia conference at Ormond College in Melbourne University in 2000 referred to the Reverend James Jefferis, an early South Australian supporter of federation who saw its achievement as a victory in religious terms: 'a liberal and generous people have demanded and obtained a free church in a free state', which he saw as the basis of a more just social order. How the churches and other religious organisations use their freedom is itself an important issue. The extent to which they use that freedom to buy time for a church in decline, use the time to preserve the institutional paraphernalia as opposed to focusing on preaching the gospel and living in truth. The risk implied in faith is about forsaking survival strategies in favour of a lived and demonstrable faith.

There is still much to be learnt from Reinhold Niebuhr, who was probably the last significant and influential commentator on politics from a theological perspective in Washington. Niebuhr was no amateur fiddling with politics, rather a Christian seeking within his tradition 'to establish the connections between human experience, social fact and biblical symbol that make these judgements possible'. Hauerwas is critical of Niebuhr and those who seek to find common language, middle axioms in which to address the human condition. His criticisms are important because the danger for any political commentator (eg Tim Costello, Frank Brennan) is that while they often speak on behalf of Christians and the church they are not facing the church when they do so. The danger is that they may speak in the name of principles or attitudes which are not subject to any theological rigour, which may not be owned by the same churches which they claim to represent. Niebuhr's approach, so Lovin argues, neither relies on abstract principles of love and justice nor on the church's capacity to demonstrate love and justice in practice. Rather, 'a realistic faith links human aspirations, social facts and religious belief in ways that relate us to the real conditions of life, avoiding exaggerated expectations and debilitating hopefulness' (Lovin, 1995, p 104).

The emphasis on a balance between beliefs and experience seems to me to be very important in linking faith to politics. The strength of Niebuhr was in his understanding of human nature. He was able to grasp the ambiguities and contradictions implicit in human nature and at the same to time embrace the possibility of the resolution of conflict and the possibility of hope. He also had considerable knowledge and understanding of the many issues on which he commented in *Christianity and Crisis* over so many years.

In the 1960s and '70s there were in inner city ministries around Australia many younger clergy and other church workers who I think saw the importance of bringing together human experience, social fact, and biblical symbols. These themes were significant in the formation in 1969 of the Fitzroy Ecumenical Centre for Urban Research and Action (CURA). This centre echoed in its life the much broader themes of the ecumenical movement at this time of a just participatory and sustainable society. It stressed more than perhaps any other centre of its kind in Australia at that time the importance of research and an informed understanding of the issues it addressed. While the centre was local, its vision was much broader, and together with other church-based ministries in the inner city CURA was able to make a major and I would argue enduring impact on the inner city in Melbourne. Even more importantly, as Mark Lopez (2001) has recently shown in his important study of the origins of multiculturalism, this centre together with the rather more specialised Ecumenical Migration Centre (EMC) had a major influence on the development of multiculturalism in Australia as a policy which was to win bipartisan support at the political level. Certainly through my experiences with EMC and CURA I came to understand the importance of a grounded approach to policy formation and in that an approach to politics which would be oriented towards the importance of doing more than protest, rather the importance of setting agendas in place.

In summary, the task of the church is to be a community of integrity. Its programs and services are important, but not as ends in themselves. They need to express the tension of those who live in two worlds at once. There are dangers in churches seeing themselves primarily as welfare agencies or, even more seriously, seeking to offset decline through increasingly contracting with the state social services for which the state is ultimately responsible. The churches in addressing society increasingly need to recognise the need to take into account the reality of cultural and religious pluralism. On the one hand, when the church's offer services they should be seen in terms of the church's mission in the world.

This allows me to move on to the third question, which is about vision and agendas.

Politicians are always enjoined to demonstrate vision, some sense of the future and how they would shape it given the opportunity. I imagine the same is true of leaders of the churches. Churches and political parties now put much more emphasis on analysing public opinion through polling, focus groups etc. Hugh McKay this weekend has been briefing the National Council of Churches in Melbourne on the results of the opinion polling research that he does. The Christian Research Association similarly does this kind of work for the churches.

There are limits to the value of this kind of research, although it can be very suggestive For example, Hugh McKay's book *Generations* suggests that we think in terms of the life cycle and life formation that is focused rather more on the longer term than focusing so much on what is happening to people at a particular point in time. This is important because it allows us to think about people in terms of all the ups and downs of their lives. It would seems to me that this is also more consistent with the sense of life as being a journey in which we have to make choices and decisions, face various challenges, with the periods of transition representing often the greatest threat and the greatest opportunities.

I have just been at Queens College in Melbourne (Conference of the Australian Theological Forum[1]) thinking about the nation, its history and religious values. This was a follow-up conference to that which I have mentioned earlier. In this conference we have been thinking about the centenary of federation from various angles. How important has the influence of the churches been over our history? What can we learn from that history? A number of generations of Australians have come and gone over this period and we as a nation have faced various challenges. Paul Kelly's book *The End of Certainty* is largely about the 1980s, but it does encourage us to think about social values at the turn of the century and then to think about our values now. I have thought about this comparison in part as a challenge to political imagination. Perhaps concentrating more on the post Second World War period as reflecting a period in which there was a social settlement based on full employment and a commitment to building a society free of the uncertainty which had characterised the pre-war period.

Australia as it enters a new century faces significant challenges if we are going to be able to build a just, participatory and sustainable society. I express those challenges as social and environmental, but of course they also require sustainable economic policies. Public policy by its nature crosses disciplines and functional areas.

Justice and sustainability in the post-war period were very much the product of full employment based on families supported by male bread winners, 'the wage earners welfare state'. Our economy was less open and based on Keynesian economic policies, emphasising economic growth as a major policy objective. The economy was strongly protected by various tariff barriers, emphasised the role of the state and saw economic growth as the principal means of maintaining full employment. This model of the economy came apart in the 1970s largely due to international influences which today we describe as the onset of globalisation. The pressures on Australia were to build the base of a new economy.

The shift towards a more open economy has resulted in ongoing structural change and realignments, which has seen the collapse of full

---

1. Held in July 2001 and entitled 'Spirit of Australia: Religion in Citizenship and National Life'.

employment. While the economy gets the most attention, there have also been very important changes in the way that we live, with the post-war image of the nuclear family in the suburbs becoming less and less representative of Australian households. Gradually it has been recognised that it is not as if the Australian economy has not been growing and the numbers of jobs have not been increasing. There have also been important changes in the way that work is distributed. The post-war full employment had been based on the male bread winner family which had been in place since federation, with a sharp distinction between paid and unpaid work. The workforce was a very male workforce, working in goods-producing industries. The shifting emphasis on information and service industries has favoured the employment of more women. It has also redistributed jobs and wealth in Australia.

The shift towards a more open and more international economy has been associated with a shift in values and in the way that people live, whether at home and or at work. Flexibility has become the buzz word, with people required to cope with frequent if not constant changes. These changes have already had massive impacts, which we see in higher and longer-term unemployment. Families are also subject to much more change and are far less settled. In this situation the certainty which was emphasised in the post-war period as the value which promised to replace the uncertainties of the depression and war-time period has largely gone. There is now much greater emphasis on helping people to cope with and to manage risk.

These changes in the nature of work and the much greater diversity we see in families are not all negatives. Consider the very high rates of part-time work. One in four workers is now part-time, and this reflects the much higher rates of female participation in the workforce and often a choice to balance the need to earn additional income and manage caring responsibilities. Apart from economic necessity, this trend for many women, even with younger children, provides a clear choice to seek to combine home and a career.

It is important at a time in which our society is changing in very fundamental ways to try to come to terms with these changes around the concerns and values which seem to be the most important. The changing nature of work and its implications for family seems to me to be an important theme with immense importance for the future of this society. The hours of work are no longer diminishing but the average hours of work are increasing, with a certain percentage of the workforce working more than fifty hours a week. On the other hand, there are hundreds of thousands of households which have no adult in the workforce. More than a million children are growing up in households where there is no adult in the workforce. More and more children and younger people are being raised in households where there is no partner to assist by providing income or by assisting with caring. Whereas employers were seen by Justice Higgins at the beginning of the twentieth century to have responsibilities for families, today families are not the concern of employers, who may place pressures on people to work hours in shifts that are not sensitive to families and family life.

These changes in work and family life are not of merely passing importance. Their impact will be felt across the life course and will be associated with wider changes in the way that younger people approach maturity and older people age. There are already appearing very different patterns in child bearing, with the lowest fertility rates for a century. Forty per cent of marriages will not survive and increasing percentages of people will live alone. The focus on individual success in managing risk will work for some, who will do well, but many will not do well in this information economy and networked age into which we are now entering.

I am not sure how much influence religious groups will have on the issues to do with globalisation, although I have been impressed by the dialogues organised by the Archbishop of Canterbury with the World Bank on its most recent world development report. The World Council of Churches has been involved in discussions with the United Nations, and an Australian Christian John Langmore has spearheaded the UN summit on poverty held in Geneva (Copenhagen) in 2001 and battles to try to get some control over international investment to accelerate the effort against poverty. I think that, more modestly in Australia, the churches might seek to initiate some study of the trends in work and their implications for families and living patterns—not in some attempt to return to the past, but rather in emphasising ways of ensuring the compatibility of work and family life in the future. This is a considerable challenge in Australia, where so much of our policy formation is done incrementally and where we make so little attempt to plan the policies for the future. The churches should resist the tendency to look at what they have done in the past or might do in the future as being of marginal importance. The frequent references to social capital should remind people how important churches were in building communities in post-war multicultural Australia. Few institutions were more important than churches in building the post-war suburbs, indeed in building the basis of civil society. The churches will be important in building communities in which the relationship between home and work is undergoing a significant transformation. However, the future will require very different policies than applied in the post-war period. The churches have a very important part in seeking to understand and then responding to the challenges that lie ahead.

References

Berger, Peter L, *The Noise of Solemn Assemblies* (Doubleday and Co, 1961).

Black, Rufus, 'Theology and the Private, the Personal and the Public', in *Interface: A Forum for Theology in the World*, Vol 3, No. 1, March 2000:

Borg, Marcus J, *Meeting Jesus Again for the First Time* (Harper, 1994).

Cox Harvey, *The New Reformation* (London: SCM Press, 1965).

Hauerwas, Stanley, *Resident Aliens: Life in the Christian Colony* (New York: Abingdon Press 1989).

Kelly, Paul, *The End of Certainty: Power Politics and Business in Australia* (Allen and Unwin, 1994).

Lopez, Mark, *The Origins of Multiculturalism in Australian Politics 1945–1975* (Melbourne: Melbourne University Press, 2000).

Lovin, Robin, *Reinhold Niebuhr and Christian Realism* (Cambridge: Cambridge University Press, 1995).

McKay, Hugh, *Generations* (Sydney: McMillan, 1997).

Robinson, John, *Honest To God* (London: SCM, 1963).

Spong, John Shelby, *Here I Stand: My Struggle in Christianity for Integrity, Love and Equality* (San Francisco: Harper Collins, 2000).

Webber, George, *God's Colony in Man's World* (New York: Abingdon Press, 1960).

The Gospel and Globalisation

James Haire

In approaching this issue, and its consequences, we go back in the first instance to the New Testament experiences of the gospel, that is, the total 'Christ event', and of its communication. The Christ event took place within an immediate Jewish cultural environment, surrounded by an Aramaic and Hebrew vocabulary and Semitic expectations. Yet this integrated Judaism, in its strict and official vesture, rejected Jesus of Nazareth, and later turned against Paul in his championing of freedom from the law through Jesus Christ. In fact, the impact of the Christian message on strictly integrated Jewish culture was minimal. On the other hand, although the events at Athens in Acts 17 show us that the initial impact of integrated Hellenistic culture was equally limited, the general penetration into Hellenistic culture in the years ahead was far more marked. Moreover, in fact from the earliest days there was already some impact, in that Hellenism was a far more loosely organised culture than Judaism, and in the mixtures of Hellenism with other cultures, particularly Hellenistic Judaism, the Christian message found acceptance.[1]

Although, of course, there was an *Anknupfüngspunkt*—point of contact—between the Christ event and Jewish culture, in another sense there was a greater *Anknupfüngspunkt* with Graeco-Roman culture. More than Judaism, this latter culture was more a 'culture' in the original sense of that word; that is to say, it was related to primarily agricultural societies in the sense that their deepest concerns in ordering their lives were attuned to being in harmony with nature.[2] For this reason an event in which were involved the elements of birth and death and resurrection, and of suffering and healing, all related to the divine, was likely to have immediate importance.

In this way, then, we can see the spread of the gospel into the Graeco-Roman world. However, although a similar situation had

1. See for example Acts 13: 13–52; 18: 1–17; 28: 16–28
2. See the wider concepts in Niebuhr, *passim*; see too Tillich, 61–125.

existed in the traditions of the prophets and psalms with their dreams of destruction and rebirth, in general first and second century Judaism presented a very different concept of culture; in this there was no drama of the earlier type, but rather the precise following of particular divinely inspired words which had been uttered up until the time of Ezra and the 'men of the great synagogue' and thereafter had ceased in such a way.[3] Thus, for example, in relation to law, the Graeco-Roman understanding of jurisprudence was related to the natural and cyclic order, while the law in Judaism was related more to clear and fixed divine interventions and ordinances.[4] It was in the natural and cyclic culture of Hellenism and its successors, rather than in the word and ordinance culture of Judaism, that the gospel or the Christ event eventually came about in its initial widespread manifestation. Of course, it was the Greek language in which the Christian message found its written expression.[5] However, the matter was not only that, but was much deeper than that; for behind, for example, the adoption of Roman juridical concepts was not only the facilitating of communicating the import of the Christ event but also the beginning of the transfiguration of this culture through the interworking of Christ event concepts and the understanding of natural and cyclic order.[6]

This interworking of the gospel and the 'culture of nature' has until recent times been a dominant strand in the expansion of the church. For many centuries the church continued to live in the successors of Graeco-Roman culture. From time to time its modes of expressing the Christ event were slightly adjusted to suit changing moods, but in general Europe, where the issue was most manifest, was evangelised through the gradual (although sometimes halting) assimilation of its varying cultures into the now firmly established catholic Christian culture. So in Europe the transfiguration of agricultural society meant that the gospel was both totally interwoven into the fabric of the culture and also itself moulded and directed the cyclic and nature-

---

3. As in the first words of the 'Pirqê Abôth'; see Danby.
4. See Aristotle, Ars Rhetorica, I. 13, 1373 b.; Testament of the XII Patriarchs. Judah 26: 1, in Charles.
5. For example, the Platonism in Hebrews 1:3; the Stoicism in Romans 1:18–32.
6. On this, see Quell, 1964, and Schrenk, 1964, where dikaiosuné (cf the goddess Diké) is seen as part of the natural order (eg Plato, *Res Publica* IV, 433c. ff).

related impulses of the culture. Wholeness, harmony, rhythm and ritual (in water or around a thanksgiving meal) were also both the medium and the message.

However, in contrast to the European, and specifically the Latin, growth of the gospel, the response in Judaism and later in middle eastern Islam was small. The culture of a mobile people engaged in bartering and exchange and the search for wealth needed common verbal ordinances to bind it together. Pre-eminently in Islam the Arabic text of the Koran was the normative rule of faith and life. In Islam the prophet Muhammad was more rigidly related to the divine ordinances in verbal form than the eighth and seventh sentury prophets of the Old Testament with their dramatic stories and symbolism.[7] In this it may indeed be said that, on the day around AD/CE 49 when the council at Jerusalem decided to follow Paul's line, the relationships of the gospel to the future Latin West and Muslim Middle East had been set.

In the West the breakdown of medieval catholic Christian culture coincided with the expansion of travel and trade. The breakdown was, of course, not total, in that this earlier culture has remained too in Europe until recent times. However, the journeying individuals and communities needed clear-cut ordinances in their dangers and temptations, far from the cyclic life of the soil which was in their eyes so clearly transfigured by the Christ event. Thus from the time of the Reformation there was the emphasis on the 'Book' (Bible), the Guide to the Book (Catechism) and the 'Interpreter' of the 'Book' (Preacher). There was, in fact, a tendency to a cultural mode similar to that of Judaism and Islam; as the emphasis on the Bible related to the respective emphases on the Torah and the Koran, so the emphasis on a catechism related to the respective emphases on the Mishnah and Talmud and the Sari'ah, and the emphasis on a preacher to the emphases on a rabbi and a faqih. Nevertheless, there was a significant difference. The various Reformation traditions were all originally rooted in the Latin culture of the natural order, and only came under the influence of the mercantile word-culture as they moved out of the original agricultural societies.

The biggest wrench from the old order came with the mass movements across the Atlantic, but even here in certain circumstances

---

7. For example Amos 7: 1–6, 13–15.

there was not a complete wrench as agricultural societies were formed again in the New World.[8] Nevertheless, one of the societies early to take advantage of the enormous opportunities available in trade and journeying was that particularly in the western and northern parts of the present-day Netherlands. The evidence of this to this day is in the widely scattered place-names: Staten Island in New York (formerly Nieuw Amsterdam); New Zealand (Nieuw Zealand); Arnhem Land (Northern Australia); Tasmania; and Transvaal. It was in these areas, among others, that strident word-cultures developed, with the Christ event both interwoven into this new fabric and directing the impulses of this new culture in Western Europe. In this it is significant that it was the presbytery (*Classis*) of mercantile Amsterdam which early arranged for ministers (*Ziekentroosters*) to accompany ships for the crew's comfort. This emphasis on comforting and guiding in potentially hazardous circumstances is a hallmark of a word-culture.

Relative to the size of its population, the Netherlands was probably more directly involved in movement, exchange and search for valuable metals and merchandise over a longer period of time than any other European nation. The other contender, of course, would be the United Kingdom; however, the number of British administrative or mercantile personnel posted overseas, for example, for a colonial territory, was relatively much smaller. In this it is significant that not only was the highpoint of Calvinism as a word-culture held at Dordrecht on Netherlands soil but also two strictly word-culture forms of Dutch Christianity were set up in the United States and South Africa. The movement and danger here were more significant than that, eg life in Michigan or the Transvaal involved farming too. In those areas the ties with the Latin nature-culture of Europe had been so severed, and the necessities of a word-culture so instilled in the need for courage in facing new adventure, in the need for guidance in uncharted travel and in the need for ordered communal living for those from diverse backgrounds, that the Reformed tradition as mediated from the Netherlands in each of these two continents became in large measure a fully integrated but monolithic system. Of course, such movements took place not only from the Netherlands but also from the other European trading societies, particularly in the United Kingdom.

8. See Troeltsch, 665–6.

Where these mass-movements of word-cultures took place, taking with them their own assimilations of the Christ event, there seems to have been great difficulty in penetrating the cultures faced. Just as Judaism and Islam were structures hard to enter, so often the colonial Protestant traditions were fortresses hard to leave. So in the West Indies and the southern state of America the local population was enslaved or slaves imported, and they simply acquiesced to the colonists' religion; in Australia and mid-America a disinterested minority of the population was left after mass-extermination; in China, Japan and India the population was antagonised against Christianity.[9]

Thus we have seen the varied interactions between the nature-cultures and word-cultures, particularly in relation to the interweaving of the Christ event into them and the moulding by the Christ event of them. The history of European colonial expansion before the nineteenth century in particular is also the history of unconscious intercultural theological action, although often of a very negative type.[10]

From this we can widen the discussion to see that a church which the Christ event has been primarily related to a nature-culture needs the struggle and tension with the divine graceful criticism of that transfiguration in order to be *semper reformanda.* Equally a church in which this event has been primarily related to a word-culture needs the constant struggle with the divine fact of creation that God has placed his church in an *oikoumene* in which the basis of life is connected with a nature-culture. It is perhaps because the Christ event can never exclusively be identified either with one culture or one type of culture that Paul employs the ambiguous term *he akoe* to describe the action by which the Christ event enters a person's or a community's life, that is, the crucial step that leads to faith.[11] For in a sense, in either of the two types of cultures in which the gospel lives just described, that gospel or Christ event must become pagan in the original meaning of that term,

---

9. See Boyd, 117–119.

10. That is, either of the nature (Portuguese, for example) or word (Dutch, for example) type. Although the Portuguese and Spanish were involved in trading, of course, in the late fifteenth and early sixteenth centuries, their ties were still very much with nature cultures at home, and their early expeditions more forays from the homeland.

11. See Taylor, 254. See, for example, Romans 10:16–17; Galatians 3:2.

and yet must also be under the opposing divine criticism; this, in fact, is seen in the varied theologies in the New Testament.[12]

The implications for Australia

I want now to look at the question of how what we have seen above may be applied in practical terms within our Australian context. It is not my intention to attempt to make an analysis of all those terms which are associated with Australian identity. By that I mean I do not intend to look in a comprehensive way at all terms like 'mateship', 'secularism', 'egalitarianism', 'our convict origins', 'the search for the good life', and so on. I do not think it appropriate at this point to look at these particular items in detail, because in recent years there has been considerable debate as to whether each of them really is of significance in relation to the Australian community of the 1990s, and to what extent they are. Nevertheless, I wish to draw out from this analysis of cyclic- or nature-culture on the one hand, and book-culture on the other hand, a number of issues which I consider to have specific importance in the Australian context. It seems to me that an analysis of Australian society needs to be carried out against the categories of nature- or cyclic- culture and of book-culture. It seems to me further that the Australian society which I see in some areas represents say seventy per cent cyclic-culture and thirty per cent book-culture, in other areas perhaps eighty per cent cyclic-culture and twenty per cent book-culture, and in other areas perhaps fifty per cent cyclic-culture and fifty per cent book-culture. In other words, it seems to me that in our Australian context both of these factors are of extreme importance and are in a variety of combinations according to locality. Let me for a moment give you one example. Many observers coming from overseas see in Australian suburbia a protest against being in a city. That is to say, the way in which housing is arranged is done in order that those who live in the houses may so far as possible try to avoid being identified with the city, even though they live within twenty-five or thirty minutes' drive of the heart of the city. That kind of analysis suggests that a combination of cyclic-culture and book-culture are clearly necessary in areas like that. Therefore, the areas with highest percentages of cyclic-culture may not necessarily only be in the country. They may also be in the outer suburbs of the major Australian

12. See also for example, Käsemann, 1951–52, and Käsemann, 1952–53.

cities. Therefore, what I am saying is that the cyclic-culture analysis may have major importance in relation to the dwellers in the metropolitan areas, ie the analysis in relation to cyclic-culture has an impact on a very large section of the population. It seems to me that for the evangelism of any part of this country it is extremely important for parish councils, ministers, presbyteries, dioceses and clergy to work out the percentage of book-culture and cyclic-culture within their bounds and to bear that in mind as they plan their evangelism, witness, ministry and wider service.

In relation to this, I would like to point to four factors in the Australian context which I believe are important, and which relate to cyclic-culture and to book-culture. They are: first—celebration; second—community; third—egalitarianism; fourth—the importance of restricted groups. The first two relate to nature- or cyclic-culture, and the second two relate to book-culture. As I have said above, it is important in the Australian context to realise that combinations of the two cultures provide the background to the situation in each particular area, although the percentages vary from place to place.

The Christ event must live in, and yet transfigure, the culture in which it is placed, always at the same time struggling with the fact that it is the divine which has entered this world. The authentic 'gospel' or Christ-event-for-us is not prepackaged by cultural particularity but is living. The church is the acceptance of the Christ event within its particular culture in each place, and yet in the wrestling with that which stands against its own particular acceptance in each place it is called to be both catholic and ecumenical and reformed and yet reforming.

References

Aristole (Aristotelis), *Ars Rhetorica* (Scriptorum Classicorum Bibliotheca Oxoniensis), edited by WD Ross (Oxford: Clarendon Press, 1959).

Boyd, RHS, *India and the Latin Captivity of the Church: The Cultural Context of the Gospel*, Monograph Supplement to *The Scottish Journal of Theology*, No. 3 (London: Cambridge University Press, 1974).

Charles, RH, editor, *The Testament of the Twelve Patriarchs* (translated by the editor from his Greek text, and edited), 'The Testament of Judah, the fourth son of Jacob and Leah' (London: Adam and Charles Black, 1908), 68–99.

Danby, H, *The Mishnah* (translated from the Hebrew by H Danby), 'The Fathers' ('Pirqê Abôth'), (Oxford: Clarendon Press, 1933), 446–461.

Käsemann, E, 'Bergrundet det neutestamentliche Kanon die Einheit der Kirche?', in *Evangelische Theologie*, Munchen, Volume XI, 1951/52: 13–21. Subsequently published in E Kãsemann, *Exegetische Versuche und Besinnungen*, Erster Band, 2nd edition edition (Vandenhoeck und Ruprecht, Gottingen, 1960).

Käsemann, E, 'Zum Thema der Nichtobejektivierbarkeit', in *Evangelische Theologie*, Munchen, Volume XII, 1952/53: 455–466. Subsequently published in Kãsemann, 1960.

Kittel, G, editor, *Theologisches Worterbuch zum Neuen Testament* (English translation: GW Bromiley, editor, *Theological Dictionary of the New Testament*) (Stuttgart: W Kohlhammer Verlag, 1933).

Niebuhr, HR, *Christ and Culture* (New York: Harper and Brothers, Publishers, 1952).

Quell, G, 'Concept of Law in the Old Testament' under 'δκη', in Kittel, English translation (Grand Rapids: Eerdmans, 1964), 174–178.

Schrenk, G, article on 'δικη', etc, in Kittel, English translation (Grand Rapids: Eerdmans, 1964), 178–225.

Taylor, JV, *The Growth of the Church in Buganda: An Attempt at Understanding* (London: SCM Press 1951).

Tillich, P, *The Protestant Era*, translated and edited by JL Adams (London: Nisbet and Company, Ltd, 1951).

Troeltsch, E, *The Social Teaching of the Christian Churches*, translated by O Wyon, Volume II (London/New York: George Allen and Unwin Ltd/The Macmillan Company, 1931).

Global Citizenship or Global Irrelevance?

Reflections on Mainstream Western Christianity and the Emergence of International Civil Society

Allan Patience

1. Introduction

The broad—although still necessarily opaque—vision behind this essay is of a reimagined and revivified Christianity that is able to play a role in shaping 'globalisation'. The plethora of old and new experiences that we currently shove under that rubbery rubric has so far eluded any single theoretical, philosophical or theological system. Undigested theory has yet to catch up with the myriad globalising practices unfolding in the world. Is it about the decline of state sovereignty? Do these events herald the birth of global governance? Is it merely an 'information revolution', via the Internet? It is about the spread of universal free markets on the road to an 'open' global economy? Is it simply an international political adjustment to the end of the Cold War? Is it the beginning of a multicultural dialogue between the world's great religio-cultural traditions? Is it a 'clash of civilisations'?

However we try to imagine it, globalisation quickly escapes from our reductive conceptualisations to take on a vast and as yet incomprehensible life of its own. What is clear is that we must be very careful not to underestimate the radical transformations that globalisation is setting in train around the world. Nor must we underestimate the profound opportunities it is providing, for us now, and for future generations, to think stirring new thoughts and inspiring new visions about how we want to configure our states, economies, and societies to advance the dignity and wellbeing of all humanity.

But to imagine that mainstream Western Christianity (henceforth MWC)[1] can play an influencing role in these transformations may be a

1. I acknowledge that MWC is a large catch-all category. In this context it includes churches with established ecclesiastical hierarchies in Europe, North America,

forlorn hope, given its growing cultural and institutional irrelevance in the face of the complex internationalising forces that are daily being unleashed by late modernity's globalisation revolution. I shall outline later what I mean by this by referring to the role of the Vatican in contemporary global developments.

Throughout the modern era MWC has long been compromised by its pusillanimous spiritual responses to modernity's empirico-realism (or scientism), by its complacent sanctioning of Western states and the 'Western system of power',[2] and more recently by its failure to engage with the nihilo-narcissism of the postmodern moment. At best MWC has a marginal voice in the major international debates about globalisation. This is in contrast to contemporary mainstream Islam which is increasingly being attended to, with interest and with growing respect, in many influential global conversations *outside the West*.[3]

---

and Australia and New Zealand that accept the absolute control of the papacy in the Vatican (the so-called 'Roman Catholic Church' in the West). The phrase also includes the various (increasingly fragmented) Anglican (or Episcopal) communions in the UK, the US, Canada, Australia and New Zealand that, more or less (increasingly less if the Archbishop of Sydney has his way), acknowledge the spiritual leadership of the Archbishop of Canterbury. It includes the Uniting Church in Australia and related churches in the UK, the US, Canada, and New Zealand. These churches all have historical foundations and institutionalised structures (eg parishes, administrative and advocacy agencies, welfare organisations, schools and in some cases universities) that can give them significant political and cultural influence. I do not include under this rubric the more 'Bible-centred' churches like the Southern Baptists in the USA, or charismatic and ultra-proselytising churches like the Assemblies of God, Seventh Day Adventists, Mormons, Jehovah Witnesses, etc because they are more often than not collaborative with a highly populist approach to their cultures, hence they are inherently oppositional to globalisation.

2. See, for example, Ralph Miliband, *The State in Capitalist Society* (London: Weidenfeld and Nicolson, 1969).
3. Contemporary mainstream Islam is not to be confused with fundamentalist Islamism. 'Contemporary mainstream Islam' refers to thinking that is impressively evident in writers like: Syed Muhammad Naquib Al-Attas, *Islam and Secularism* (Kuala Lumpur: ISTAC, 1993); Anwar Ibrahim, *The Asian Renaissance* (Singapore: Times International, 1996); Edward Said, *Peace and Its Discontents* (New York: Vintage, 1996); Ahmed S Akbar, *Postmodernism and Islam* (London: Routledge, 1996); Bobby Sayyid, *Fundamental Fear* (London:

If MWC is going to help shape the new international civil society now unfolding, it will need to find ways of contributing authoritatively, yet humbly and inclusively to 'the making of global citizenship'.[4] This is one of the most promising and progressive forces at work in the contemporary world. As late-modernity begins to exit from the global stage, MWC is in grave danger of exiting with it, and for similar reasons. The advent of global civil society is challenging modernity as it has never been challenged before. Along with it, under serious challenge, are a whole lot of peripheral institutions that have clung to its ruling elite's coat-tails and sung in its nostalgic choruses. These include liberal capitalist markets, conventional military forces, self-serving professional groups (eg doctors, lawyers), adversarial employers' organisations, combative trade unions, mass media monopolies, and narrowly secularist cultural institutions. Right among these peripheral institutions are the diverse, ageing, and shrinking associations and institutions that contribute to the contemporary retiring character of MWC.

Indeed, it may be argued that what we are witnessing here is not only the transformation of these institutions through globalisation, but also the death of some of them—including (or especially) MWC. For those who nonetheless still align themselves with a broad Christian ethic (as outlined below) it may be they will not feel the necessity to mourn the death of the old MWC. Instead, they will anticipate its

---

Zed Books, 1997); Bassam Tibi, *The Challenge of Fundamentalism* (Berkley: California University Press, 1998); Ali Mirseppassi, *Intellectual Discourses and the Politics of Modernization* (Cambridge: Cambridge University Press, 2000); Susan Buck-Morss, *Thinking Past Terror* (London; Verso, 2003); *The Middle East and Islam World Reader*, edited by Marvin Gettleman and Stuart Schaar (New York: Grove, 2003). On Islamism and fundamentalism see, for example, Hedley Bull, 'The Revolt Against the West', in *The Expansion of International Society,* edited by Hedley Bull and Adam Watson (Oxford: Oxford University Press, 1984); Abdulrahman Kurdi, *The Islamic State* (London: Mansell, 1988); Youssef Choueiri, *Islamic Fundamentalism* (Boston: Twayne, 1990); John Esposito, *The Islamic Threat* (New York: Oxford University Press, 1992); Leslie Lipson, *The Ethical Crises of Civilization* (London: Sage, 1993); Tibi (1998); R Scott Appleby, *Strong Religions* (Chicago: Chicago University Press, 2003).

4. Richard Falk, 'The Making of Global Citizenship', in *Global Visions,* edited by Jeremy Brecher et al (Montreal: Black Rose Press.

resurrection, in new, collaborative, and inclusive forms in a momentously creative globalising context.

2. Globalisation

Princeton's Richard Falk has proposed two very broad ways of approaching an understanding of globalisation. He thinks of globalisation (as do many writers on the subject) as an experience as old as humanity itself. It has taken on a revived intensity and some remarkable new forms since the 'ending' of the Cold War (circa 1989).[5] This intensifying has been happening in the wake of the revolution-ising global transformations emanating from the swift spread of the world wide web (the Internet), the linked portentous growth in mass media and information networks, and momentous increases in human global mobility (eg through tourism, migration, international business and educational exchanges, the worryingly rapid growth in refugees and people-smuggling activities, military mobilisations, and terrorism).

2.1 'Predatory globalisation' (PG)

The first—and very negative—approach to globalisation that Falk identifies is 'predatory globalisation' (henceforth PG).[6] This is the kind of globalisation that motivates (and often enrages) the thousands of activists demonstrating against international meetings of the representatives of world money markets and multi- and transnational corporations and their associated agencies (including some powerful states like the USA and the European Union).

PG is all about the rich world, with a mercilessly influential military-industrial complex at its core, getting exponentially richer, at appalling cost to the rest of the world. It is a world in which some twenty per cent of the world's population (who mostly live in 'advanced' or liberal-capitalist economies in countries like the US, in the European Union and Australia) monopolises and consumes more than eigthy per cent of the world's resources (food, energy, water, housing, technical knowledge, medicines, arable space, etc). It is a world in which the three largest stockholders in Microsoft possess

---

5. R Falk, 'The Making of Global Citizenship'; Richard Falk, *Predatory Globalization* (Cambridge: Polity Press, 1999).
6. Falk, *PG*.

more capital than the combined resources of all the peoples of Africa. It is a world of appalling inequality and distributional failure, in which some 40,000 children die every day from illnesses directly attributable to malnutrition.[7] It is a world that corrals butter and cheese mountains in Europe, or thousands of kilos of wheat in silos in the USA and Australia, to keep market prices high, even as people starve in other parts of the world. It is a world in which multinational pharmaceutical companies refuse to open their patents or sell their life-saving drugs to the poor world because they make massive profits by selling to the sick —and not-so-sick—in the rich world. It is a world in which rich governments subsidise highly inefficient and environmentally dangerous farming practices (eg cotton farming in the USA and Australia) to be able to compete unjustly against farmers growing cotton—far more cheaply and efficiently—in very poor states (eg in Africa). It is a world where evils such as poverty, starvation and pandemics (many of them humanly contrived) stalk the majority of people on a daily basis.

PG contributes to the making of a world in which most people, most of the time, are denied access to even the most basic levels of justice and security. It locks them out of any kind of adequate representation in the highest councils of the world. It leaves them without any legal avenues to fight for global equity and justice. It is precisely within this brutalising and unequal world that grim responses and desperate acts become all but inevitable. We, who by sheer good fortune live in that part of the world that is well off, condemn all too easily the desperate reactions of those outside our complacent comfort zones. These reactions—bitterness, frustration, anger, violence, fanaticism, insurgency, terrorism, jihad, war—become all but reasonable when we closely and frankly examine the circumstances giving rise to them.

2.2 Globalization-from-below (GBF)

The second form of globalisation that Falk identifies is 'globalisation-from-below' (henceforth, GFB).[8] As Professor Singer explains: '. . . now we are beginning to live in a global community'.

---

7. D Rosati, 'The Limits of Openness', in *Globalization*, edited by Isabelle Grundberg and Sarbuland Khan (Tokyo: United Nations University Press, 2000).
8. Falk, 'The Making of Global Citizenship'.

> Almost all the nations of the world have reached a binding agreement about their greenhouse emissions. The global economy has given rise to the World Trade Organization, the World Bank, and the International Monetary fund, institutions that take on, if imperfectly, some functions of global governance. An international criminal court is beginning its work. Changing ideas about military intervention for humanitarian purposes show we are in the process of developing a global community to protect citizens of states that cannot or will not protect them from massacre or genocide.[9]

As Singer is suggesting, GFB is based on a growing global consciousness of the common fate that humans share globally. This consciousness is a significant result of the so-called 'information revolution' that is central to all forms of contemporary globalisation. It is a consequence of the ever-expanding Internet, the massive growth in mass media networks, and the momentous increases in global human mobility. The result is a world becoming increasingly intimate with itself.

GFB contributes to a world in which alterities—othernesses, strangenesses, differences, alternative ways of interpreting being and actually being—slowly but surely become unthreateningly familiar in communally pluralistic or multicultural settings. The very great value of these settings is that they provide us with opportunities to see 'others' as ourselves, the 'I' and 'thou' as 'we' and 'us'. They offer us glimpses of our potential selves writ differently, alternatively, interestingly, maybe even riskily or confrontingly, and sometimes with great vivid drama.

Using a very useful religious metaphor here, GFB's growing global intimacy arises from people coming to understand and appreciate that most human differences (at individual, socioeconomic, political, religio-cultural and global levels) are vivid and equally valid reflections of the multi-complexity of the Creator. Most traditions and most persons (or 'selves') within each tradition are thus partial revelations—representations—of the ultimate Whole. Each thus

---

9. Peter Singer, *One World* (New Haven: Yale University Press, 2002), 196–167.

deserves an ultimate form of respect and empathy. However, this is not to argue that *all* individual or socio-cultural differences are *always and equally* valid representations of the Creator. But presumably a Christian response will always be to act in good faith, lovingly, in 'acting' to discern the 'other's' 'authenticity'. If the discernment is prolonged and problematic, presumably the Christian is obliged to act in good faith (walk the extra mile, turn the other cheek), and if at the end of the day s/he is proved to have discerned wrongly, nonetheless in good faith, the *only* response can be 'Amen'.[10]

Nor is this to suggest that there should be no cultural or political changes in the world. As GFB grows, so will influences and forces for global cultural change, some positive and others that will need sensitive interrogation and negotiation. Nowhere is this more dramatically and encouragingly evident than in the considerable gains made by international women's movements and international environmentalist movements. While much has yet to be achieved, the gains already made by such movements make it clear that there will be no going back to a world order based exclusively on patriarchy or environmental and climatological destruction. Those evil days are well and truly over—even as we acknowledge that we still have a still distant future to win on these (and other) issues. Win it we shall. But this is going to require the close international cooperation and continued activism of women, men, gays, lesbians and transgendered people, and people who love the earth and its flora and fauna, together with those religio-cultural leaders and other political and intellectual leaders who understand the profound import of a freely and fearlessly multigendered and clean world. This cooperation and activism are one of the major features of an emergent international civil society —one, incidentally, that mostly operates well outside the institutions of MWC.

3. Civil society

Reflecting their Cold War origins, many modern discourses on civil society have tended to emphasise the adversarial relationship, or

---

10. See Karol Wojtyla (Pope John Paul II), *The Acting Person* (Dordrecht: Reidl, 1979); Charles Taylor, *The Ethics of Authenticity* (Cambridge MA: Harvard University Press, 1994); Charles Taylor, *Sources of the Self* (Cambridge: Cambridge University Press, 1989).

tension, that exists between the sociopolitical apparatuses of modern states (governments, bureaucracies, repressive or authoritarian agencies like secret police, prisons, para-military forces, propaganda units, and related 'official' institutions) and the social associations and institutions and individuals over which the state exercises what Max Weber described as a monopoly of legitimate (or 'legal') force. It is these social associations and institutions, and the individuals who make up their memberships, which are conventionally given the term 'civil society'. Bratton, for example, argues that civil society operates in the interstices between the state and the family—in that public-but-not-political domain that is not immediately of the state, but neither does it intrude in the private context of the domestic sphere. It happens outside, or beyond, the things we normally see as 'political' (ie attaching to or emanating from the state). But most importantly, it is the major source of democratic legitimacy for the truly democratic state.[11]

Community service organisations, trade unions, recreation groups, sports clubs, book clubs, choirs and repertory groups, hobby circles, groups of public intellectuals, a free media, parents and friends organisations, etc all contribute to the development of robust civil society.[12] The more active the civil society, the more democratic the state will be, provided civil society values the benefits that a democratic state can provide.

Democratic governance can only be nurtured and expanded where there is an intimate and open relationship between the state and civil society—where there exists what has been appropriately termed a 'civic culture'.[13] The repressive apparatuses of the state are kept in check by maintaining a strict separation between the major branches of government (legislature, executive and judiciary)[14] and (often) via a constitutionally entrenched bill of rights. Citizens have regular and

11. Michael Bratton, 'Beyond the State', *World Politics,* Vol 41, No. 3, 1989: 51–81. See also Michael Bratton, 'Civil Society and Political Transition in Africa', in *Civil Society and the State in Africa,* edited by John Harbeson et al (Boulder: Rienner, 1994). See also Joel Migdal, *State in Society* (Cambridge: Cambridge University Press, 2001).

12. Robert Putnam, *Making Democracy Work* (Princeton: Princeton University Press).

13. Gabriel Almond and Sidney Verba, *The Civic Culture* (London: Sage, 1989).

14. MJC Vile, *Constitutionalism and the Separation of Powers,* second edition (New York: Liberty Fund, 1998).

uncorrupted opportunities (regular elections) to replace governments through free, secret and well-run ballots. Citizens believe—and often act accordingly—that they not only have the *right* to replace governments that have lost their confidence, but (as John Locke proposed) also the *duty* to replace them.[15]

Totalitarian and/or authoritarian governance arises where there is a breakdown in the relationship between the state and civil society. The state undermines civil society's countervailing energies and institutions and ends up cannibalising them. As Hannah Arendt pointed out, in her classic comparative study of Nazism and Stalinism,[16] totalitarian states 'atomise' civil society through fear and propaganda campaigns and the increasingly unbridled uses of coercive measures (eg internal security acts, as in contemporary Singapore and Malaysia). As they become more and more atomised—ie separated out from associations and institutions (even families) that could provide a bulwark or hedge against state intervention and state power—so people become subject to the authoritarian/totalitarian state, they become vulnerable to state-sponsored intimidation and repression. In this context civil society soon dies unless it can be kept alive by leaders with moral courage and public intellectuals who will articulate and fight its causes.

4. International civil society

As noted above, GBF is a new and promising version of civil society. The growth of this society is often in direct contradiction to the state in international political arenas.[17] It underpins a growing realisation that sovereign states are often limited in what they can do to guarantee the security of their citizens. As Dupont[18] has shown, in many contexts

---

15. Dennis Thompson, *The Democratic Citizen* (Cambridge: Cambridge University Press, 1970); Carole Pateman, *Participation and Democratic Theory* (Cambridge: Cambridge University Press, 1976).
16. Hannah Arendt, *The Origins of Totalitarianism* (New York: Harcourt Brace, 1973).
17. Three excellent recent accounts are: Alejandro Colas, *International Civil Society* (Cambridge: Polity Press, 2002); Mary Kaldor, *Global Civil Society* (Cambridge: Polity Press, 2003); John Keane, *Global Civil Society?* (Cambridge: Cambridge University Press, 2003).
18. Alan Dupont, *East Asia Imperilled* (Cambridge: Cambridge University Press).

today states are simply incapable of coping with threats to their citizens' security because of the transnational nature of those threats —eg global warming, HIV/AIDS, SARS, international drug cartels, international crime syndicates, Internet hackers, terrorists. And as the ICISS Report shows, a majority of states in the world today are often incapable of protecting their citizens against these kinds of security threats.[19]

At the same time, we are increasingly conscious of the ways in which states are structured to minimise democratic citizenship by configuring power into the hands of elites and privileged interests. In the large or 'advanced' states there is much derisory talk of 'failing' or 'weak' states that are riddled by corruption and incompetence and which often constitute a major source of their own people's insecurity.[20] For example, recent comments by Australian government officials about problematic states like the Solomon Islands or Papua New Guinea reflect an inappropriate self-confidence that glosses over the fact that it is not just small, struggling post-colonial states that are problematic when it comes to the nurturing of democratic governance. For example, a recent study of American citizens' views about how their system of government should work demonstrates (alarmingly) that only a very small minority of US voters have any serious and knowledgeable commitment to their democratic institutions.[21]

Increasingly, then, states *per se* are being seen by many activists as sinister or incompetent agencies that may have to be transcended in order to achieve global democratic governance.[22]

Furthermore, the emergent global civil society under survey here is a root and branch contradiction of the threatened 'clash of civilisations' scenario so grimly prophesied (or grimly advocated) by Samuel

19. International Commission on Intervention and State Sovereignty, *The Responsibility to Protect*— www.dfait-maeci.gc.ca/iciss/report-en.asp

20. See, eg, Michael Handel, *Weak States in the International System* (London: ass).

21. John Hibbing and Elizabeth Thiess-Morse, *Stealth Democracy* (Cambridge: Cambridge University Press, 2002).

22. See, for example, *Cosmopolitan Democracy,* edited by Daniele Archibugi and David Held (Oxford: Blackwell, 1995); *Governing Globalization,* edited by David Held and Anthony McGrew (Cambridge: Polity Press, 2002). See also Singer, *One World.*

Huntington.[23] Like some orthodox Christian ideologues in the past, Huntington thinks of non-Western religio-cultural traditions (or what he ambiguously calls 'civilisations') as inherently conflictual, even primitive. He prefers to paint them wildly, as primordial fundamentalisms mired in populist hatreds and dangerous irrationalities. Where he departs from orthodox Christianity is his assertion that only Western secular rationalism can permanently underpin liberal-democratic forms of governance and their contingent, relatively orderly and advanced—or advancing—societies. From his rather nostalgic perspective, the United States of America represents the most modern, most advanced, the most liberal-democratic achievement known to humankind. We could beg to differ . . .

The intellectual leadership of the emergent global civil society rejects Huntington's dogmatic late-modernist discourse. It calls for self-awareness and, simultaneously, a profound empathy for the 'authenticity' of other peoples, other cultures, other traditions. It advocates a dynamic form of multiculturalism, one that is constituted by what Charles Taylor refers to as 'the politics of recognition'.[24] This is a radical intellectual departure from the pro-Western secular and Christian orthodoxies of the past. But it can be seen to resonate with a more generous, less 'realist', less salient Christian ethical discourse, one that has moved along subtly in the background to mainstream church institutions and their once powerful central structures and agencies.

Viewed from contemporary globalising perspectives, openness to other religio-cultural traditions has not been noticeably evident at the core of the MWC and the ideological and institutional orthodoxies that underpin it. Their institutional histories are generally characterised by opportunistic alliances with Machiavellian elites and hierarchies. These histories entail proselytising crusades, monstrous pogroms, and savage inquisitions—most of them directed against the 'other', the 'heathen', the 'alien', the 'stranger' for whom the choices are simply conversion

---

23. Samuel P Huntington, *The Clash of Civilizations* (New York: Simon and Schuster, 1996).
24. Charles Taylor, 'The Politics of Recognition', in *Multiculturalism: Examining the Politics of Recognition,* edited by Amy Gutmann (Princeton: Princeton University Press, 1993); Charles Taylor, *The Ethics of Authenticity;* Charles Taylor, *Sources of the Self.*

or condemnation and often death by the (Christian) sword or crusade. And Western Christianity's close links with the ruthlessness of Europe's imperialisms leave it with a powerfully negative legacy among those today who long for, and who are now often actively working towards, a post-colonial, globalising and democratising world. In short, Western Christianity's institutionalised histories are sometimes very ugly and often deeply shameful. They are prominently —and properly—fixed in the consciousness of those who are contributing to the making of today's global citizenship.

The contemporary transglobal movements contributing to the advent of an international civil society constitute a major reaction against the agents of PG. It is richly inspired by visions of universal human rights, international cooperation, and global justice. It is true that many of these visions are half-baked and not infrequently plagued with internal contradictions. But they are nonetheless compelling because there are few, if any, inspiring moral alternatives. There are today no widely influential and inspiring moral accounts of goodness, mercy, compassion, love, care, or altruistic concern readily and meaningfully available to a world that is becoming more nihilistic and narcissistic by the minute. Our world today is one in which 'predatory globalisation', with all its talk of neo-liberal economics (free trade agreement, open markets, level playing fields), tightens its ruthless grip on the world's poor and vulnerable.

This is a world urgently requiring what Professor Singer's refers to as an 'ethics of globalisation'.[25] But Singer doesn't imagine for a minute that there is a useful role for MWC. He sees it playing no role at all in articulating a moral defence of democratic forms of world governance, vastly widened categories of human rights, increased global peace-making and peace-keeping operations, and effective programs aimed at achieving greater global economic equality and social justice. This may be viewed by recalcitrant church figures as Singer's problem, but it is far more MWC's problem. In the sometimes ethically awesome workings of global bodies like the United Nations and its agencies (eg UNESCO, UNICEF, the International Criminal Court) and major international NGOs (eg the International Committee of the Red Cross, Oxfam, Greenpeace) the institutionalised Western church is more noteworthy for its absence than its influential pro-active participation.

---

25. Singer, *One World.*

While there are some splendid church-based global aid and relief agencies, they do not have the widespread moral force or ethical authority of the non-church international NGOs. This point is even more strongly evident if we note the church's apparent irrelevance in the trailblazing 2001 Report of the International Commission on Intervention and State Sovereignty. As noted in its introduction:

> The report's central theme is 'The Responsibility to Protect', the idea that sovereign states have a responsibility to protect their own citizens from avoidable catastrophe, but that when they are unwilling or unable to do so, that responsibility must be borne by the broader community of states. We hope very much that the report will break new ground in a way that helps generate a new international consensus on these issues.[26]

At no stage does the report advocate a constructive role for MWC *per se* in the making and maintaining of this absolutely vital international consensus. The implicit assumption appears to be that it is either passé, or irrelevant—perhaps both.

Much of the nascent global civil society leadership is idealistic and optimistic. But it is nearly always deeply distrustful of corporate and bureaucratic power structures that manage established global interest groups and their provincial or local agents. And these provincial and local agents include states. The history that is driving international civil society away from MWC, and which is provoking a growing repugnance, especially among younger international activists and leaders, is associated with a deep and justifiable antipathy towards the old world 'order' involving superpower rivalries, big power bullying, transnational corporate greed, and fragmenting nationalisms and patriotisms. This sensibility is evident in Susan Buck-Morss's words:

> We coexist immanently, within the same discursive space but without mutual comprehension, lacking the shared cultural apparatus necessary to sustain sociability. We are in the same boat pulling against

26. *The Responsibility to Protect*, Introduction.

> each other and causing enormous harm to the material shell that sustains us. But there is no Archimedean point in space in which we could station ourselves while putting the globe into dry-dock for repairs—no option, then, except the slow and painful task of radically open communication that does not presume that we already know where we stand.[27]

United in opposition to worsening global inequality, the leaders of today's emergent global civil society are also variously struggling against 'transnational' threats to human security that include HIV /AIDS and SARS, global warming and climate change, attacks (including attacks by increasing numbers of modern states backed by corporatist interests) on human rights and freedoms, internationally organised crime (eg drugs, sex slavery, piracy, and people smuggling), the deliberate constraining of people's access to clean water, food, medicines, housing, education.[28] On a number of these issues (eg HIV/AIDS) some mainstream churches are equivocatory at best and pusillanimous at worst.

5. The Vatican

An unfortunately vivid illustration of what I mean by the irrelevance of MWC in the contemporary context of globalisation is the role of the Vatican in the late-modern Catholic Church. This 'universal' Catholic Church is dominated by a Vatican bureaucracy intent on accruing and monopolising power and maintaining an exclusive, authoritative and ultimate say in all moral, theological and organisational—hence political—matters affecting the 'Church' (by which is usually meant the unquestioned and unquestionable primacy of the Vatican and its institutional backbone of appointed and privileged cardinals and bishops). In this respect the Vatican is, as it makes clear itself, a late modern authoritarian state, with all the limitations of state power structures in a globalising world.

This example of authoritarian church structuring (one that is increasingly a model for other mainstream 'conservative'—or 'neo-conservative'—Christian churches around the world) is now widely

27. Buck-Morss, *Thinking Past Terror*, 6.

28. See, for example, Dupont, *East Asia Imperilled*.

viewed as exercising immense and threatening control over a compliant or cowed hierarchy and an increasingly disillusioned global laity—much as totalitarian states dominate their various functionaries and subjects, demanding abject obedience over individual conscience and personal moral responsibility.[29]

As a result, the emergent international civil society is beginning to pass the Vatican by as it moves forward into a global future.

For example, the Vatican is seen by many progressive global activists as being in active opposition to the growth of international civil society—that it would, if it could, strangle it at birth, as if it were some latter-day Herod. This is painfully evident, for example in Vatican diplomacy at United Nations' conferences canvassing women's rights and equality in private and public life—including the right to actively and openly debate issues like women's health, women's access to proper financial support, and access to effective and safe birth control and abortion procedures. In these forums the Vatican has joined with some extremely dubious states, some of which are ruthlessly authoritarian—especially towards women—in an effort to stall progressive policies for global female equality. Equally disturbing are strenuous Vatican efforts to thwart World Health Organization strategies designed to combat the spread of HIV/AIDS—through, for example, public education programs advocating condom use as part of safe-sex practices. These WHO programs are especially targeted in Africa where the spread of HIV/AIDS is a major killer. Vatican spokesman Cardinal Trajillo is on the public record declaring that it is 'scientific fact' that the HIV/AIDS virus can pass through micro-pores in latex rubber condoms, hence condoms are useless in the fight against the spread of that murderous virus.[30] The subsequent Vatican position is to urge chastity and/or marital fidelity as the only solutions to stopping the spread of HIV/AIDS. To say that this is a naïve view in a late-modern world is putting it mildly. Mostly it is seen to be what it really is—a case of tragic ignorance.

---

29. See, for example, Paul Collins, *Papal Power* (Melbourne: HarperCollins, 2000); Thomas Reese SJ, *Inside the Vatican* (Cambridge MA: Harvard University Press, 1996).

30. For a comprehensive report, see Pamela Bone, 'In the fight against AIDS, Catholics can only be ashamed', *The Age*, 1 December 2003.

It may not necessarily be a bad thing if all we see of the Vatican is its ugly history, its contemporary institutional arrogance, its cozying up to the agents of 'predatory globalisation'. That kind of MWC deserves to be abandoned and despised. It is irrelevant to the broader forces of GBF and this will become increasingly obvious as time moves forward.

But there are still those inspired by the sublime Christian ethic of self-abnegating love, of grace-inspired and enabled altruism, of loving others as we ourselves would be loved. This admittedly dwindling band within the faltering institutions of MWC is acutely conscious that the contemporary globalising era lacks any meaningful articulation of the uniquely *Christian* ethic—or ethos—of unconditional love. It knows little of turning the other cheek, of doing unto others what we would have done to us, of walking the extra mile, of surrendering also one's coat if one's shirt is asked for. It is barely aware of the enormous moral challenge to love and privately pray for our enemies, because that is what God invites us to do in order to overcome our 'misrecognition' of our enemies, to recover from our inability to 'recognise' their 'authenticities'.[31]

Arguably, a persuasive and intelligent articulation of this intensely demanding moral ideal is needed now more than at any other time. A loveless globalisation—a world without charity in the richest sense of that over-used but under-comprehended word—is a global nightmare. A world devoid of love means unconditional surrender to a very modern and corrosive narcissism and nihilism. The result could well be the spread of terrorism worldwide—and *that*, almost certainly, will plunge us into a universal holocaust, into the ultimate realisation of Thomas Hobbes' 'war of all against all'.

6. Conclusion

We need to unpack what is meant by globalisation and 'international civil society' to show that globalisation does not need to be seen as a threat to a Christianity that is open to a loving dialogue with the world around it. This essay is intended as a small contribution to just that kind of Christianity—one that is not closed in its late-modern structuring, but open and able to walk with integrity and optimism into a

---

31. See Taylor, 'The Politics of Recognition'; Taylor, *The Ethics of Authenticty.*

promising global future. We now need Christian leaders who will be prepared to walk away from the old, often nostalgically imagined MWC of the pre-globalisation past and who can take us forward into the globalising future. The challenge is as exciting as it vast and highly risky. And so is the way of the cross.

Part III

Welfare Perspectives

Church and Civil Society: Social Compact

Linda Campbell

The way current services are expected to operate: a children's, youth and family services perspective

I have been asked to reflect upon some of the issues I see emerging in the church-sponsored services to children, young people and families with which I am familiar. My perspective is that of an insider to this 'industry' but an outsider to the churches. My comments come from my involvement with and observation of a number of agencies over the years as worker , evaluator, educator and board member. I am not, however, representing anyone, and I make no pretensions to entering your theological debates. Indeed, to an extent I have to take your assurance that there are entities called churches seeking to engage with 'society' through the vehicle of church-sponsored agencies, in any other way than institutional sponsorship arrangements, in which the parties exchange symbolic goods to earn legitimacy. I remain a little puzzled about these relationships.

1. Some background

Children's and family services have, as you will be aware, long been provided by church agencies, with an especially rich set in Victoria. This dates back to pre-pension times, when church orphanages provided as much for children of the living poor as for orphans, taking them both on a voluntary basis and via the state arrangements for apprehending and arranging care for destitute children. These old children's homes can be seen as having set some of the early foundations for today's complex church-state-agency terms of engagement. In many sites, costs were heavily subsidised by the cheap labour of religious orders, and the death of the facilities was a product not only of policy changes around standards of child care but also driven by the decline in this labour bank and the costly process of industrialisation of the workforce. This set us on a path towards ever-increasing professionalisation and cost in child and family services, with the church agencies themselves pressuring government to fully fund services that became defined as residual responsibilities of the state, contracted out to the non-government sector. At the same time as professionalising some aspects of service, the church-sponsored agencies drew on their community connections and volunteer resources to establish a much more widespread foster-care system. Increasingly, these people provided much of the direct child care, while professionals became responsible for managing the systems and providing direct assistance, counselling and the like to parents in need.

After a flurry of activity in the 1970s, many of these preventive and therapeutic services struggled to attain a secure funding base, and the legacy of this tenuous grip on a share of the government funds is still evident in the degree of agency contribution many agencies have to make to this work.

Throughout the latter decades of the twenteith century we saw a dance of approach and avoidance between state and church agencies: the agencies claiming higher levels of funding from the state (indeed, argued for a hundred per cent), the government demanding more accountability in return, and the agencies countering that increased standards required increased funding. This dance continues, and all parties have contributed to its choreography. It could be argued that the symbiosis between the state and the agencies tends to be stronger than the symbiosis between the agencies and the church.

Through these processes, there have been lots of questions about what is whose core business. The case of foster care has been an interesting example, with some major shifts over time, from a 1970s ideal of a new kind of foster care that would strengthen families and communities through family-to-family engagement in local communities, respite in times of trouble, and expanded social networks, to a system heavily oriented to intensive, protracted and costly services to children under statutory court orders. With the explosive redefinition of family troubles as child protection matters from the early 1980s, these backbone services of the church family welfare agencies have become more and more closely tied into the imperatives of the statutory child protection system.

Over time, it could be argued, this has led to something of a mission dilution and creep. While service ticks along quite well, and still provides a wonderful link between church, state and fellow citizens, there is increasing concern about exploiting volunteer commitment, and demeaning families who have to use these services. We are at risk of stopping at the minimum level of service provision—child safety and people moving. Outcomes like family dignity, a child's experience of joy, parental sense of social and intrinsic value, become incidental by-products, rather than core goals. I am not sure what foster care outcomes local parishioners might desire and support, but the major referrers want 'good bed occupancy rates'. This strikes at the heart of foster care as a voluntary act of altruism, reciprocity or citizenship.

2. Current government rhetoric and policy

In Victoria, the Community Care Division of the Department of Human Services, the major tune-caller for the child, youth and family services, has recently proposed objectives that would be hard to reject, under the banner of stronger citizens, stronger families, and stronger communities.

The planning framework they have put up focuses on early intervention, both in terms of the stage in the family life-cycle, and in terms of averting problems before they become entrenched. Nevertheless, responsibility for the 'hard core' remains with the state and is in turn delegated to the non-government agencies. In addition, the government seeks to be much more responsive than it has been to both Indigenous communities and the wide array of culturally and linguistically diverse communities. These have not necessarily been well served in the past by traditional church agencies. Beneath all this lies an expectation of continuous quality improvement. Non-government agencies, including church-sponsored agencies, are asked to work 'in partnership' with government to achieve these objectives.

This invitation to partnership is a more pleasing challenge than the previous culture of competition, but is no less a challenge, if only because competition continues to lurk beneath the surface. What partnership might mean—in the sense of mutual and equal contributions and benefits—is not really clear even between agency and government, let alone between agency, government and church.

3. Key dilemmas

The agencies confront some key dilemmas in proceeding with child and family services development. Each agency has its own history and skill and resource bases against which to consider these choices. Among the choices to be made are those about where to locate themselves along what has been described repeatedly as a continuum of service from prevention to protection and remediation.

4. Where to focus their effort?

4.1 *Focus on the prevention/early intervention end?*
This has a lot of appeal . . . scope for engaging professional enthusiasm and job satisfaction; reaching out to a wide range of ordinary families in the community and helping them get off to a good start; building on existing skills in communities, in parishes, where a lot is understood about local living conditions and demographics; linking in to the reserves of positive family life already going on in the community and building on existing networks of support and mutual aid; promoting 'feel good' values about family life. Some of this is the sort of work local government used to do and could conceivably do again. Choosing this focus has some immediate practical drawbacks—it wastes some of the existing expertise, is potentially boundaryless, crosses over into the turf of other systems (kinders, maternal and child health), and to be really effective requires a massive development of links with the systems that provide other fundamentals of community life—education, employment, housing , local industry etc. And there are no guarantees about preventing serious social malfunctioning in families to a level that would leave agencies comfortable in totally withdrawing from the remedial end of the continuum.

4.2 *Maybe focus on families and young people who are showing significant signs of distress?*
This picks up available professional skills and knowledge, builds on what is there, has a known steady level of demand, still has the satisfactions of preventive work, fits with the needs revealed by a lot of front-line professionals in the community, teachers, clergy etc. It is very client-centred work, needing to proceed at a client's own pace. Church-based agencies can be very good at doing this work, but have some major challenges on their hands to secure adequate funding for

services that are sufficiently flexible and open-ended to allow families to get what they need, when they need it, and as often as they need it.

It strains against the target-driven assumptions of economic rationalism, even though superficially it is relatively easy to package up as 'case management' work, with nice clear objectives, timelines and outcome measures. The problem is that this work will reveal wider community issues and needs that will require attention, but may get ignored in the steady flow-through of routine direct service. It's a limiting way of engaging with and influencing the larger questions of civic society.

4.3 Maybe focus on those in most trouble?

This is consistent with the traditional missions of many of the agencies that have maintained a high commitment to the outsiders, the growing band of seriously disturbed citizens . . . the abusive and neglectful parents; the violent partners; the children out of control; the self and other harming, slash and burn adolescents; the suicidal and alienated. This choice makes use of existing technologies, and the state is desperate for the work to be done but it is getting harder and harder to deliver, is more and more challenging to the volunteer contingent. It is also a money pit, an ever-absorbent dollar sponge, and not always attractive to the benevolent dollar or corporate sponsorship. Nothing is ever good enough. This work brings drama, moral dilemmas, public censure, scandals.

The quality challenges are enormous. And the work can be profoundly disturbing for staff, who need real sustenance in their roles.

So where to focus? No easy answers. Agencies and their church affiliates need to be talking and thinking about how these foci fit with their place in their communities. A major practical problem is that these apparently discrete functions are not in fact discrete—families move along the supposed continuum, and live their own lives with scant respect to conceptual and bureaucratic distinctions. They need to dip in and out of services with trusted and accessible workers.

5. Some issues to consider in moving forward

- *Locality matters*. While we live in a global world, children still need to reared in particular times and places. Services need to be on a scale families can approach without fear. They need to be embedded in the life of local communities, well-connected to the forces of mutual support and regulation. It might be argued that parishes are natural partners in this work, but so are schools and other child-size institutions.

- *Planning matters*. There's more than enough work to go around, and agencies do differ. They should have some freedom to negotiate according to location, expertise, credibility, in a rational way. For church agencies to compete on a winner-takes-all basis puts them at risk of recreating state bureaucracies with all their inherent dilemmas . . . who wants it?

- *Mature dialogue between key stakeholders*. It strikes me as interesting that some churches seem to be wanting to pull their welfare offspring back into the family business just when they have matured in their own businesses. (I may have mistaken the direction—perhaps the agencies themselves have scurried back to the parental nest.) But because they have been divergent, the relationships are up for renegotiation. Just as I have had to renegotiate both my relationships with my children as they grow to be autonomous adults, and my own understanding of my world in the light of their new interpretations of it, so I would expect the churches to enter into dialogue about what the agencies have learnt in their forays into the otherwise hidden homes and streets of a distressed society. But similarly, just as I ask my adult children to conduct the dialogue with respect to some shared values—and to my great relief find them still there—so I would expect the agencies too to be examining what they hold in common with the church actors who seek more engagement with society through the agency.

Some of the common ground I think I have seen is pretty obvious, but how it is built on may still be contested. Common ground seems to include a desire to assist people to free themselves from abuse and exploitation, both as victims and perpetrators; an interest in building pathways to social participation for people who are unbelievably alone and excluded; an interest in building family-friendly communities: safe places to walk, talk, watch the kids, share.

Churches and their agencies clearly borrow from the legitimacy of the other. While agencies can benefit from the moral standing of the church in the community, this is by no means always clearcut. Similarly, while churches can benefit from the evidence of active work in the society, it comes at the cost of controversy. Agencies have grown to be professional, responsible, complex. They have to be competent and procedurally impeccable employers; to have stringent financial control; to be highly accountable in multiple directions. They are engaged with a larger set of stake-holders, with the church auspice being just one. Meanwhile, the work done is complex, moral, fraught with decision-making moments, often deeply distressing. At worst, the people seen are often dislocated and impoverished, feel profoundly worthless, and project great anger on all and sundry. In the past, workers have often found the churches have not assisted them to grapple with these issues. The relationships between agencies and churches need therefore to be developed sensitively, and I am hearing of some real efforts on both sides to do so.

Such efforts include modestly broadening the base of governance and advisory structures to facilitate more vigorous debate, widening the volunteer opportunities to accommodate a wide range of interests, talent and availability offered by local parishes. Some managers report local clergy and congregation offering real practical, emotional and pastoral support to themselves and their staff in the issues they face. Agency staff make efforts to go out and speak with church groups, offer services, debate issues, support initiatives, even though this is all accommodated within highly pressured workloads. To push the dialogue further may mean both more growth and more conflict . . . avoidance is sometimes easier. There are some fundamental questions encountered in welfare that will always elicit a divided response, among them gender roles, drug use, homosexuality, abortion, even child discipline.

But to attempt to claim a tighter relationship between church and agency requires that the realities of the work to be done are explored. It is conceivable that for some churches and congregations, these services may not be the preferred site for their engagement in social issues.

6. Conclusion

Despite the potential for conflict, to me, the core goals for children, young people and families engaged with these services hinge around the less contentious issues of nurturing children, building social connectedness and just distribution of social resources.

These are goals have been at least ostensibly shared by successive governments, and not inimical to the foundations of the churches. I think that one of the present tasks for these agencies is to slow down and take a hard look from the perspective of the disadvantaged clients who rely on these institutions. Do the programs that have been developed for achieving those ends sufficiently preserve compassionate and just processes? Do they make best use of the combined public and private resources—material and human—available from the sometimes uneasy coalition of secular and religious interests? From the churches' side, it may still be worth asking to what extent this field, which has had its own existence internationally for over a century, can and should be regarded as the work of the church, or an allied, parallel human phenomenon.

Church and Civil Society: Rules of Engagement

Joe Caddy

Central to Christian belief is the assertion that Jesus came as a man amongst women and men to inaugurate the reign of God. Followers of Jesus are called with others to be instruments of transformation in our world so that it may more and more reveal and reflect God's realm. God's realm breaks into and transforms the world wherever fear is transformed into love, bitterness into forgiveness, deafness of heart into receptivity, blindness of vision into clarity, total despair into unimagined hope.

To be true to their mission, it is essential for Christians that they engage with the world in which they live. It is not enough for them to relate solely or even chiefly to some other heavenly world where they do not live. The life of Jesus as presented to us in the gospels reveals a couple of aspects about the way in which Christian engagement with the world ought to be promoted.

For a start, the gospels present Jesus as a person who was willing to engage with anybody. He would speak to them, listen to them, enter their homes and dine with them. They were people from various races and traditions, of varying political beliefs, the wealthy and powerful, the poor, those who were sick, those who were excluded, untouchables and sinners.

Secondly, Jesus through his own actions reveals that in God's greater scheme of things nobody ought to be excluded from the broader sense of engagement that makes up our social networks. Jesus consistently brings from the edges back to the centre those that were estranged, excluded or marginalised.

- The ten with leprosy are sent back into the city from the edges of the town where they were excluded as unclean.
- The woman caught in adultery is brought from the brink of death and the accusation of the mob to the new position where no one condemns her.

- The prodigal son, who has seemingly excluded himself through his own behaviour is in fact embraced on his return and is brought to the centre of his father's household, where he is revered as the one who was lost and has been found. His more judgmental brother did not approve. But it is the father in the story who models God's love and judgment.
- Again, the shepherd will leave the ninety-nine to go in search of the lost sheep. Many would have seen and been touched by the beautiful image of the good shepherd who carries the lost one back to the fold.

Although not necessarily motivated by the same tradition and sense of mission, it is this same worthy desire to bring back to the centre those who have been excluded that motivates the concern of many in government and in the community sector to work with those who are disadvantaged and marginalised.

The question then is one of policy: what is the best way to go about re-engaging those who have been excluded?

One group that has been excluded from much of the economic and social activity in Australia over recent years has been the long-term unemployed. How have our broader society and our social policies engaged them in the search for their greater sense of participation and inclusion?

Unemployment is undoubtedly the main cause of poverty in Australia. In June 2001, according to Australian Bureau of Statistics (ABS) figures (which are acknowledged by many to grossly underestimate the real extent of unemployment and underemployment), 680,000 people were looking for work.

Of even greater concern, however, is the fact that according to the Department of Family and Community Services, in September 2000, 385,000 people had been receiving unemployment-related benefits for more than twelve months, and a great proportion of them for a far longer period.

In some age groups and in some regions the figures relating to long-term unemployment are much higher and so there have emerged neighbourhoods and regions of real long-term disadvantage and exclusion.

While those with work have for the main part been able to share in the high and sustained levels of growth of income and wealth experienced in Australia over the past decade, those individuals and families that have experienced long-term unemployment have been consigned to income security payments that are set at barely subsistence levels. And so while the economy has in a general sense moved forward, those disadvantaged communities have fallen relatively further and further behind.

In response to sustained levels of long-term unemployment, the government has, through its jobs network provided intensive assistance programs which help to train long-term unemployed people and make them work-ready. For those who face even more severe barriers to employment, the Community Support Program (renamed as the Personal Support Program and allocated greater resources in the last Commonwealth budget) has allowed service providers to do some excellent work with a number of highly disadvantaged and marginalised persons. However, there is nothing like 385,000 places available under these assistance programs, and so the vast majority of long-term unemployed are forced to settle for the 'fall-back' position of a 'Work for the Dole' placement. The 'Work for the Dole' scheme has been expanded enormously over recent years. Along with other approved activities it has increasingly been used as one of the conditions under which people are allowed to receive an income security payment. The mechanism used to enforce these activities is a harsh and rigorously applied system whereby those who do not comply are 'breached' and have their income security payments either severely reduced or stopped altogether.

The activities themselves are principally designed to change the behaviour of long-term unemployed or disadvantaged people, on the assumption that if they change they will be able to gain access to paid work and other opportunities. Admittedly 'Work for the Dole' has been improved since its earlier days and now much better addresses the need for training, and with the introduction of training credits announced in the last budget will do so to an even greater extent in the future.

However, the assumption still seems to be that an improvement in the supply of labour will lead to an increase in the demand for labour. This dubious assumption underpins much of welfare reform and denies the reality that for every job vacancy there are at least seven or eight jobless people. It also denies some other realities, namely that there are severely disadvantaged regions and communities and that poverty and disadvantage is frequently also linked to difficulty in gaining access to decent and affordable housing, education and health care.

Endless cycles of work for the dole or training, keeping people permanently job ready and permanently on very low levels of allowance or pensions, is likely only to increase their sense of exclusion and sense of resentment. This poses a real problem that requires much clear thought. The generation of jobs must be central to any program to reduce long-term unemployment. But even this is not simple, given the realities of globalisation, markets and production techniques.

With changing technology and productivity gains, it must now be questionable as to whether full employment is required to produce the goods and services necessary to satisfy the needs of our society. If income is only distributed for work, how will we ever ensure that all people, even those who are unnecessary to the production process, receive their share and maintain their sense of place and belonging? Or are we, as a society, going to continue on the path towards the total abandonment of those who are 'non-productive' in the economic sense?

Obviously these questions and other equally important ones around social and environmental sustainability are key policy questions for us all. The search for answers calls for open and inclusive dialogue and rigorous social research.

However, it seems that there are some structures within our political and social system that work against the real engagement of a broad range of people in such discourse and leadership.

One of the structures that work against open engagement and dialogue in Australia is our adversarial political and social systems. They are such that they discourage bi-partisan approaches to big questions and encourage attacks on persons who attempt to address broader issues that may call them to take a position of leadership.

It is not only the political parties that feed into these systems; other pressure groups also understand the current rules of engagement and the sad reality that it is the one who thumps the table the loudest who is most likely to be heard.

They may be heard, but these methods of problem solving seldom achieve the best outcomes.

Look, for example, at the reaction to the reports of the recent speech of federal treasurer, Peter Costello, at the Sydney Institute.[1]

---

1. In July 2001.

From what I heard on the radio, he included in his speech some talk about 'tax mix' and was beginning an explanation as to why he believes that we need to move away from our reliance on direct taxes towards indirect.

My own view is that direct taxes are progressive in nature, while broad-based indirect taxes tend to be regressive and place an unfair burden on the poor. But from what I heard, the treasurer had some valid arguments, certainly worthy of more discussion. But what happened? The opposition spokesperson immediately made the claim that the Liberal Government intends to increase the Goods and Services Tax (GST) if it is re-elected.

Of course, it is not all one-way. In 2001 it was the prime minister and the treasurer who were saying that Labor's talk of 'rollback' on GST is proof that a Labor Government if elected will certainly increase income tax.

So instead of having a decent, rational and engaging debate about taxation and the 'tax mix', it is everyone back to his or her corner to plan the next assault.

Rather than taking risks and leading on important issues, it seems that the system encourages political parties to undertake polls and focus groups and to follow instead.

Consider, for example, the extent to which Australia is willing to compromise its human rights record in relation to refugees and asylum seekers. No doubt the official positions taken play up to the fears of much of the electorate and are popular enough amongst those voters likely to defect to 'one nation'. And so it goes.

The quick media grab, the sole focus on question time in parliament and the reliance on opinion polls mean that all too often it is 'smart politics' that wins at the expense of 'good policy'.

Consider a couple of recent examples:

- In the recent 2001 federal budget: Politically who could argue with an immediate three hundred dollar one-off payment to aged pensioners? But in terms of policy, is it wise to spend $660 million in that way over a two-week period when one recalls that the total welfare reform package was worth only $1.7 billion to be spent over four years?
- Amongst many in the electorate, 'Work for the Dole' is clearly a very popular title for the government's assistance to long-term unemployed. But the name is offensive, degrading and

pejorative of those who are forced through lack of employment to undertake activity tests in order to receive their meagre income security payments. The name of the scheme tends to target those people who do not have work and runs the risk of further dividing our sense of community by driving a wedge between those who have a job and those who do not.

- Policies that imply that it is necessary to have permanent budget surpluses and low government spending despite where we are placed on the economic cycle seem more designed to play up to the needs and fears of financial markets rather than the needs of the community.

No doubt the above examples are cases of 'smart politics', but it seems to me that 'good policy' requires a far greater degree of engagement and discourse.

It is not really fair to point the finger at party politics alone in this regard, because the same mechanisms are also at work at varying times at all levels of society, even and not surprisingly within churches.

However, it seems that there are some other rules for engagement that might emerge from reflection on the gospel and from a deeper consideration of what is humanly decent.

Some principles that present themselves for such reflection are: openness to all people; a sense of respect for the other and solidarity between people; the common good; and the requirement to deal firstly with the needs of those who are poor and disadvantaged.

These principles might well form the basis of some constructive new rules for civilised engagement and the inclusion of the many in social discourse and policy development.

Standing for Truth: Vision-driven Advocacy

Hilary Berthon and Lin Hatfield Dodds

1. Introduction

In his address to the Assembly of the Uniting Church in Australia,[1] the retiring president, James Haire, spoke of the enormous challenges facing the church. He referred to foreign policy, immigration policy and welfare policy and the demise of truth in public life. Our chief challenge, he concluded, is ' . . . to proclaim the truth of the gospel of Jesus Christ. As church—as the people of God—we are bound to stand for truth.'

How are we to stand for truth in the modern world? How can we speak of and proclaim the gospel of Jesus Christ in a society that sees security as less about ensuring all Australians have a decent life and more about increased military spending?[2] This paper explores how Uniting*Care* Australia seeks to stand for truth. Particular reference is made to Uniting*Care* Australia's work on poverty, the strategies that we have used and how these flow from our faith foundations. We also want to mention the signs of hope that we see.

2. Uniting*Care* Australia

The Uniting Church is one of the largest non-government providers of community services in the areas of aged and community care; children, youth and family; disability; employment; and across rural and remote communities. This commitment flows from our belief that God created all humankind and gave us responsibility for one another, with the

1. The Rev. Professor James Haire's retiring President's address to the 10th Assembly of the Uniting Church in Australia, 13 July 2003; accessible at: http://nat.uca.org.au/unitingjustice/issues/democracy/haireretiringspeech.htm; accessed 29 October 2003.
2. Uniting*Care* Australia and Uniting*Justice* Australia, 'Another step towards a divided Australia', Media release, 13 May 2003.

strongest having a special responsibility for the vulnerable. God invites all people to a society based on justice and right relationships.[3] In its 'Statement to the Nation' on the occasion of the Uniting Church's inauguration, the church declared:

> We affirm our eagerness to uphold basic Christian values and principles, such as the importance of every human being, the need for integrity in public life, the proclamation of truth and justice, the rights for each citizen to participate in decision-making in the community, religious liberty and personal dignity, and a concern for the welfare of the whole human race.
>
> We pledge ourselves to seek the correction of injustices wherever they occur. We will work for the eradication of poverty and racism within our society and beyond. We affirm the rights of all people to equal educational opportunities, adequate health care, freedom of speech, employment or dignity in unemployment if work is not available. We will oppose all forms of discrimination which infringe basic rights and freedoms.
>
> We will challenge values which emphasise acquisitiveness and greed in disregard of the needs of others and which encourage a higher standard of living for the privileged in the face of the daily widening gap between the rich and poor.[4]

The Uniting*Care* network gives expression to the Uniting Church's commitment to support individuals, families and communities by providing caring services. The network consists of over 400 missions and agencies across every state and territory. Uniting*Care* Australia is

---

3. Uniting*Care* Australia, *A Decent Life*, 10 September 2003, available at: http://www.unitingcare.org.au/library/policyposition/pdf/povdecentlife.pdf; accessed 10 November 2003.
4. Uniting Church in Australia, 'Statement to the Nation—Inaugural Assembly, June 1977', accessible at: http://nat.uca.org.au/resources/statements/statement1977.htm; accessed 29 October 2003.

the national body for this network. Our primary role is policy-based advocacy, with a strong focus on social justice, and a particular concern for those who are the most disadvantaged.

How does UnitingCare Australia carry out its advocacy? What are the principles upon which we seek to base our 'standing for truth'? What are the strategies that we have found to be effective?

3. Bound to each other through Christ: partnerships that embrace

Uniting*Care* Australia has consciously chosen to be driven in its advocacy by a vision for the common good arising from the theological foundations of the Uniting Church.[5] Our primary purpose is to advocate on behalf of those who are the most disadvantaged and vulnerable in our communities. We share this focus with our agencies and missions who strive to deliver services first to those who need them most.

This kind of faith-based advocacy, we believe, must be done in partnership with others. Complex and multi-layered issues such as poverty cannot be adequately addressed without building partnerships with the people and communities we exist to serve—and across the community sector, with researchers, and with government. Working with others recognises our fundamental need of each other.

Among these partners must be the people we deliver services to: their stories, experiences and aspirations are an essential part of truth telling. The life and ministry of Jesus provides a model for this inclusive approach to effecting change. He invited participation in God's work, calling the voiceless out of anonymity[6] and with questions such as, 'What do you want me to do for you?'[7] Advocacy listens to the answers to these questions, and strives for relationships of solidarity in its actions. It is a practical working out of our understanding of a God who turns to us in grace and love, initiating a relationship with us. We respond in faith, acting in love, building

---

5. Uniting*Care* Australia, *Faith Foundations*, accessible via Uniting*Care* Australia's website: www.unitingcare.org.au

6. G Gutierrez, 'Renewing the Option for the Poor', in *Liberation Theologies, Postmodernity and the Americas*, edited by D Batstone, E Mendieta, LA Lorentzen and DN Hopkins (New York: Routledge, 1997), 78, citing Mark 5: 25–34.

7. *Ibid*, citing Mark 10: 51.

relationships with each other and identifying common pain.[8] We are bound to each other through Christ.

True advocacy seeks to tell real stories about real people, or better yet, to create safe spaces for people to tell their own stories. The Christian tradition understands truth to be transforming. When people tell their own stories, speaking from their gut, the truth of their experience cuts through theoretical discourse and bureaucracy. It is empowering for the person speaking their truth. Effective advocacy is grounded in the lived experience of those we deliver services to, and grounded in our experience delivering those services. Stories are a great way to get our experience heard.

Uniting*Care* Australia's advocacy seeks to engage with policy makers and politicians. Our advocacy role with government does not consist of fronting up to politicians and saying 'please do not do that' or 'please fund this more'. It is about influencing policy and legislative formation with government, rather than picking up pieces of policies that are too broken to fix. This doesn't mean that our beliefs will not bring us into conflict with government. However, it is essential that we engage with decision-makers, always ' . . . stress[ing] the universal values which must find expression in national policies if humanity is to survive'.[9]

Uniting*Care* Australia aims to take account of what the research and evidence base tells us. What are the most promising approaches to effecting change in the lives of people who are disadvantaged? What do our service providers and those we serve say about our programs? What other innovative programs are around? At the same time, we need to be engaging with researchers, sharing our experience and contributing to research proposals. We also need to work with other providers—ecumenically and across the community sector.

---

8. 1 Corinthians 12: 26.
9. Uniting Church in Australia, 'Statement to the Nation—Inaugural Assembly, June 1977', accessible at: http://nat.uca.org.au/resources/statements/statement1977.htm; accessed 29 October 2003.

4. In relationship with others: broadening the picture

The Christian tradition (among others) understands that people have a need to participate in society. We are created in community. Uniting*Care* Australia's advocacy around poverty has focused on our vision of an inclusive society, in which all have the opportunity to participate. Our key message has been very simple: poverty exists, it's bad for everyone, and together, we can do something about it. Communal attachment is at the heart of people's sense of wellbeing. Whatever excludes people from participating in society leaves them vulnerable and at risk.

While Uniting*Care* Australia's services seek to be an expression of God's love for individuals, we must also be concerned with the policies and structures that cause or perpetuate suffering or disadvantage. Poverty cannot be entirely understood by an individualistic analysis.[10] We must take account of the body of knowledge that suggests that societies in which there is considerable inequality show lower overall levels of health and wellbeing than societies where these differences are smaller and that these socioeconomic differences show up particularly starkly in the health outcomes of poorer sections of populations. There are social and structural dimensions to poverty.

John Wesley, the founder the Methodism in the eighteenth century, not only encouraged Methodists to provide assistance to people who were poor, but also to challenge the social and economic structures that made them poor.[11] So we need to take account of the facts, striving in our advocacy for policies that will lead to the establishment of a society within which individuals may flourish.

Yet another dimension of standing for the truth within our community is how we speak about and understand ourselves—who we are and what we hope for. In this, Uniting*Care* Australia must play

---

10. R Simons, The Smith Family, (2002) *Social Innovation for Social Inclusion* (ACOSS Congress 2002: A fair and inclusive Australia).
11. Theodore Jennings, (1990) *Good News to the Poor: John Wesley's Evangelical Economics* (Nashville: Abingdon Press, 1990); Theodore Runyon, (1998) *The New Creation: John Wesley's Theology Today* (Nashville; Abingdon Press, 1988) quoted in Uniting*Care* Australia, *A Decent Life*, 10 September 2003, available at: http://www.unitingcare.org.au/library/policyposition/pdf/povdecentlife.pdf; accessed 10 November 2003.

a role. A community is a group of people who share a story[12] and our disparate stories must be shared—the experiences of Indigenous Australians, of homeless people, of people living with impairments and of the unemployed. But then we must go on to name what it is that is evil[13] and where our hope lies. This cannot be done in a coercive way by enforcing a single expression but in a way that acknowledges the diversity and worth of all and the value of our community.

5. Part of the whole: a global community

If we are concerned about the wellbeing of communities of people, we must also be concerned about the basic human rights of future generations and people everywhere. For Uniting*Care* Australia to advocate effectively, therefore, it must look at what it is to be human—what we have in common and what it means to live whole lives. Combatting poverty will involve accepting our God-given responsibility to care for one another and the totality of God's creation through the wise use of energy, the protection of the environment and the replenishment of the earth's resources.[14] We must also be aware of our global responsibilities—to be concerned 'for the welfare of all persons everywhere'.[15] While the gap between rich and poor in Australia grows greater each year,[16] the gap between the rich and

12. P Hughes, 'Social Capital and Religion in Contemporary Australia' in *Spirit of Australia II: Religion in Citizenship and National Life*, edited by Brian Howe and Philip Hughes (Adelaide: ATF Press., 2003).
13. P Hughes, (2003) 'Social Capital and Religion in Contemporary Australia' in *Spirit of Australia II: Religion in Citizenship and National Life*, edited by Brian Howe and Philip Hughes (Adelaide: ATF Press, 2003).
14. Uniting Church in Australia, 'Statement to the Nation—Inaugural Assembly, June 1977', accessible at: http://nat.uca.org.au/resources/statements/statement1977.htm; accessed 29 October 2003.
15. Uniting Church in Australia, 'Statement to the Nation—Inaugural Assembly, June 1977', accessible at: http://nat.uca.org.au/resources/statements/statement1977.htm; accessed 29 October 2003.
16. For example, ACOSS (2000) Info 211; available via www.acoss.org.au; accessed 10 November 2003.

poor globally is increasing also.[17] Uniting*Care* Australia's advocacy around poverty needs to take account of these realities. We must also look to other countries for clues—for strategies that have worked or seem to show promise.

6. An example

Uniting*Care* Australia's focused advocacy work around poverty had its origins in a national poverty forum, which took place in January 2002, at which fourteen national community service organisations came together to attempt to bring the perspective of lived experience to the public debate which had been sparked by the Smith Family/ NATSEM report[18] on poverty and the Centre for Independent Studies[19] rejoinder to it. Much grassroots action across the sector emerged from that beginning.

Uniting*Care* Australia's choice to focus its advocacy work around the overarching theme of poverty was made for a number of reasons. A Senate Community Affairs Committee Inquiry into Poverty and Financial Hardship had been set up in response to requests from across the community sector, with hearings scheduled to take place around the country in 2003. This presented an opportunity to influence national policy in this area. Together with Uniting*Justice* Australia, Uniting*Care* Australia made a submission to the Inquiry,[20] as did

---

17. United Nations Development Program (1996) Human Development Report; accessible at: http://hdr.undp.org/reports/global/1996/en/; accessed 10 November 2003.
18. The Smith Family and NATSEM, A Harding, R Lloyd and H Greenwell (November 2001) 'Financial Disadvantage in Australia 1990 to 2000: the persistence of poverty in a decade of growth'; accessible at: http://www.natsem.canberra.edu.au/pubs/poverty01.html; accessed 10 November 2003.
19. K Tsumori, P Saunders and H Hughes, 'Poor Arguments: A Response to the Smith Family Report on Poverty in Australia', in *Issue Analysis*, No 21, January 16, 2002; accessible at: http://www.cis.org.au/IssueAnalysis/ia21/IA21.htm#authors; accessed 10 November 2003.
20. Uniting*Care* Australia and Uniting*Justice* Australia (2003) 'Submission to the Australian Senate Community Affairs Committee Inquiry into Poverty and Financial Hardship'; accessible at:

many of the agencies that had participated in the January 2002 national poverty forum. There also seemed a willingness from the Federal Government to begin to address issues extending across portfolios in a holistic way. A large body of research evidence had accumulated about topics such as the relationship between poverty, childhood development and life outcomes, locational disadvantage, and inter-generational poverty. There was plenty of data to support the establishment of innovative approaches to combatting poverty. In addition, Uniting*Care* agencies and missions across the country were experiencing the human costs of poverty and disadvantage and struggling to adequately respond to expanding and increasingly complex needs.

Given that Uniting*Care's* approach to the delivery of community services is shaped by a particular concern for those who are the most disadvantaged, national advocacy on poverty is an issue that lies at the heart of what Uniting*Care* Australia exists to do. Addressing poverty provided the opportunity to look at the larger picture against which many of Uniting*Care's* clients' experiences were being formed. Many of the specific issues that Uniting*Care* is concerned with interact with poverty. This theme was incorporated into Uniting*Care* Australia's strategic plan for 2003–2004.

Uniting*Care* Australia established a national poverty working group late in 2002 to provide input into the Senate Inquiry. This working group comprised people from our national network with a wide range of experience and expertise. The lead agency was Uniting*Care* Wesley Adelaide, whose members together had expertise in policy and research, service delivery, theology and advocacy. Supporting Uniting*Care* Australia's submission to the Inquiry,[21] a series of policy position papers were prepared.[22]

The shaping idea for the papers is the notion of 'a decent life'. The Christian tradition understands that people have basic physical needs

---

http://www.unitingcare.org.au/library/submissions/InquiryPovertyandFinHardship303.pdf; accessed 10 November 2003.

21. Uniting*Care* Australia and Uniting*Justice* Australia (2003) 'Submission to the Australian Senate Community Affairs Committee Inquiry into Poverty and Financial Hardship'; accessible at: http://nat.uca.org.au/unitingjustice/resources/submissions/PovertyMar2003.doc; accessed 10 November 2003.

22. These papers can be accessed via Uniting*Care* Australia's website www.unitingcare.org.au

such as food, housing, health and clothing, but also have other needs. These include education, participating in society and contributing to the common good, intellectual, cultural and creative activity, religious activity and community, and rest and recreation. Without these, people may survive but will not flourish. We also wanted to emphasise that poverty is bad for all Australians.

The first paper, 'A Decent Life,' put the Uniting Church's case for change on issues surrounding poverty and called for a national whole-of-government partnership approach to addressing poverty. The second paper was entitled, 'Because Children Matter: Making a Case for Addressing Child Poverty in Australia', and was prepared by Uniting*Care* Burnside. Uniting*Care* Burnside is a child and family agency that provides innovative and quality programs and advocacy to break the cycle of disadvantage that affects children, young people and families in NSW. Other papers addressed poverty amongst Indigenous Australians, homelessness and employment and labour market issues. The Uniting Church's National Director for Covenanting, the Uniting Aboriginal and Islander Christian Congress (UAICC) and a range of others, both within the Uniting*Care* network and beyond, partnered with Uniting*Care* Australia to produce these.

The papers were launched at a parliamentary breakfast briefing in Canberra in September 2003. Over sixty federal ministers, shadow ministers, senators, members of parliament, key community sector and academic leaders and senior commonwealth departmental staff came to hear from our panel and receive a poverty package containing our poverty papers and a CD 'Voices of Poverty'.

The CD contains a song written for our poverty advocacy, 'Welfare State of Me',[23] and readings of excerpts from a new book called *The Lowest Rung*, by Mark Peel, where people living in Inala, Mount Druitt and Broadmeadows tell their stories. The panel who spoke at the briefing were the Rev Shayne Blackman, Uniting Aboriginal and Islander Christian Congress, Townsville; the Rev Bill Crews, Ashfield Mission, Sydney; the Rev Tim Costello, Urban Seed, Melbourne; Ms Jane Woodruff, Uniting*Care* Burnside, NSW; Ms Mary Ecuyer, service user, Uniting*Care* Burnside, NSW.

In developing and launching the papers, the Uniting Church was able to begin to proactively address a major social policy issue in a way

---

23. Song by Pete Lyon.

that is grounded in its experience in delivering services to Australians living in poverty. This has provided many opportunities to address more focused and particular issues with politicians and federal departments, such as funding streams for children's services, and the effects of structural ageing on an already stressed aged care system.

The call for a whole-of-government anti-poverty strategy, including clear goals, benchmarks and indicators, was made across the churches and the community sector. In October 2003, during national anti-poverty week, the federal opposition committed itself to work towards a national anti-poverty strategy in opposition and to deliver one in government.

In October 2003, eight national religious leaders signed a letter drafted by Uniting*Care* Australia and our partners in other agencies calling for action on this issue from the Prime Minister, John Howard, and the premiers and chief ministers. The Queensland Premier, Peter Beattie, and the Australian Capital Territory Chief Minister, Jon Stanhope, have both called on the prime minister to put the issue of addressing poverty on COAG's agenda.

The community sector is developing the networks and capacity to communicate internationally about poverty: both its effects and approaches to address it. Uniting*Care* Australia has third sector partners in Europe and North America with whom we share information, and communicate about strategies for change.

Uniting*Care* Australia's advocacy is not based solely on approaches to policy makers and politicians. We are currently working with two other national agencies in the Uniting Church, Uniting Education and Uniting*Justice* to develop a resource about poverty for use in congregations, missions and agencies. The resource will facilitate awareness raising, enquiring and study, the developing of faith-based responses and planning for practical action in relation to poverty. It will be workshopped and developed within congregations, missions and agencies.

There are signs of hope, signs that the situation might change for the people in Australia whose lives are diminished due to poverty, disadvantage and inequality. There are signs that we as a society may be prepared to make a commitment to change the way things are. As part of the whole people of God, our chief source of hope lies in our decisions to be part of standing for the truth. And this will happen as we partner with each other, as we listen, learn, relate, speak and act. This is how we will proclaim the truth of the gospel of Jesus Christ, leading us towards the vision of reconciliation that we have for the whole human race.[24]

24. Uniting Church in Australia, 'Statement to the Nation—Inaugural Assembly, June 1977', accessible at: http://nat.uca.org.au/resources/statements/statement1977.htm; accessed 29 October 2003.

The Church and Civil Society: Mission Imperatives

Ray Cleary

At the heart of the church's engagement with civil society, is the resurrection of Jesus. In the 2000 years of Christian witness, the resurrection has been proclaimed and understood in different ways, often portrayed as a 'feel good story' or a happy ending to a sad encounter. This, of course, is a gross distortion of its true meaning. The resurrection of Jesus is a unique event of hope, and the Christian gospel is more than a statement of ethical principles upon which to build a good life. 'The foolishness of God is wiser than human wisdom, and God's weaknesses stronger than human strength', said St Paul.

In the death and resurrection of Jesus, the victim, the sufferer becomes the life-giver, the one who recognises the pain and suffering experienced by others, and offers not revenge or victimisation, but rather hope, expressing the overwhelming generosity of God. In the resurrection of Jesus, there is the ongoing struggle for justice, an agenda which is both personal and social. Resurrection, the offering of hope, stands in contrast to crucifixion and offers forgiveness and new life. Our willingness to participate in God's justice means we share in the meaning of resurrection and redemption for the whole of creation. God's love and justice is the message of the cross.

The themes of justice and equality run throughout the biblical witness of God's encounter with the creation. These stories of God's encounters with the human family tell of the deep commitment for justice in the Creator's agenda for communal life—a life enriched by the values of compassion, mercy, forgiveness and reconciliation.

The ministry, death and resurrection of Jesus are the fulfilment of this promise. The cross of Christ is the sign of God's justice and compassion, freely given for the purpose of healing our own brokenness and frailty and in restoring the covenant relationship between the Creator and the creation.

Forgiveness and hope are essential core tenets of belief in the resurrection of Jesus. Forgiveness, for others and with God, is predicated on the acceptance that we ourselves need forgiveness before we can truly and fully forgive others. In the communal arena, this implies that we all have a role in righting injustice and speaking out when exploitation, hurt or diminishment against individuals or communities is caused by the actions of others. In recent times this is clearly demonstrated in our endeavours to make peace with justice with the Indigenous people of our nation.

Jesus, in his ministry and contact with those around him, practised what he preached. He sought out the rejected, engaged ordinary people, healed the sick, and reminded the leaders of the day, not only of their responsibilities, but obligation to the communities they governed and served. He dined with prostitutes and tax evaders, never compromising himself, always extending God's mercy and forgiveness. He stands as the fulfilment of the prophetic tradition of Israel, and central to the faith of Christians.

An engagement with civil society in the politics of the day has never been easy for the church, nor is it new. In the book of Acts, we read of the early struggles of the Christian community to engage with and find their place in civil society:

> Now the whole group of those who believe were one heart and soul and no-one claimed private ownership of any possessions, but everything they owned was held in common. There was not a needy person among them, for as many who owned lands and houses, sold them, and brought the proceeds of what was sold. They laid it at the Apostles' feet and it was distributed to each as had need (Acts 4: 32, 34–5).

There have been many examples in history where Christian ethics and teachings, if not always the institutional church or its agencies, have been central to many of the human struggles for a more just and compassionate community. This is evidenced by:

- The Civil Rights Movement in the United States
- The abolition of Apartheid in South Africa
- The work of Archbishop Oscar Romero in El Salvadore
- The removal of President Marcos in the Philippines.

The recent debates over how to respond to the perceived threat to the world by Iraq has seen Christian, and other religious leaders, active in opposing war and promoting peace.

In Australia, there have been many examples of the call for a more just community and the eradication of poverty, led by a coalition of churches, individual Christians in partnership with many others. Christians have been active in debates about economic and social policies. Examples of such initiatives are:

- The 1972 enquiry into poverty in Australia
- Aboriginal reconciliation
- Tax reform and the Goods and Services Tax (GST)
- Welfare reform, including the issue of mutual obligation
- The treatment of refugees and asylum seekers and
- The child poverty campaign in 1982.

Many of these initiatives have been undertaken in partnership with others. Nor is it true to say that there has been a singular theological response or understanding on such issues. The key point to note is that the Christian community has always been involved in influencing civil society.

For many Australians, the events of the past 18 months have raised serious questions about the role and place of religion in its engagement in our postmodern and multifaith secular society. In some cases, the claim is made that religion is the cause of much current unease. Questioning of this nature is not new. Faith and religion have always been challenged, and history tells the stories of how differing parts of the human community world-wide respond to the claims of faith. This is not to suggest that the church should be above criticism. On many occasions, our involvement in society has resulted in much pain and suffering.

Conflict in the Middle East and Northern Ireland come immediately to mind, but equally, disturbances between Muslims and Hindus in Asia. The present spate of terrorist attacks that have directly affected Australia, however, have heightened our sensitivity to the place of religion in a multifaith and multicultural, postmodern society. Today, many of our senior politicians, including the prime minister, have made statements challenging the church's role in engaging in political debate, claiming that the churches have no monopoly on the high moral ground.

There are many Christians today, as in previous generations, who express concern, some even outrage, when church and community leaders challenge and debate with political and corporate leaders economic and social policy which they see as victimising or marginalising sections of the community. Many reject the role of clergy and laity as social commentators, particularly when such comments are made from the pulpit.

In my own experience, I receive more criticisms of statements on issues of justice from those within the church than those outside. I am not alone in this experience. Let me quote here from *Christianity and Social Order* by William Temple:

> The claim of the Christian Church to make its voice heard in manner of politics and economics, is very widely resented, even by those who are Christian in personal belief and devotional practice. It is commonly assumed that religion is one department of life, like art or science, and that it is playing the part of the busybody when it lays down principles for the guidance of other departments, that are art and science, or business and politics.
>
> . . . Few people read much history. In an age when it is tacitly assumed that the church is concerned with another world than this, and in this with nothing but individual conduct as bearing our prospects in that other world, hardly anyone ever reads the history of the church in its exercise of political influence.
>
> It is assumed that the church exercises little influence and ought to exercise none; it is further assumed that this assumption is self-evident and has always been made by reasonable men. As a matter of fact, it is entirely modern and extremely questionable. [1]

At the same time as an increase in the questioning of the role of churches to engage in political, economic and social issues, this nation has witnessed over recent weeks a renewed search for meaning and understanding in light of the tragic and evil act of destruction and death in Bali, and the killings at Monash University. Some have

1. W Temple, *Christianity and Social Order* 1941 web edition, 5ff.

responded with the question, where will it end? Others have asked, where is God? Churches report a small number of people seeking to re-engage with a faith community. Each time a tragedy occurs, faith communities of all traditions respond, and as at the time of the Bali tragedy, have led the nation in prayer, and offered not only comfort, but raised serious issues for reflection. Many have offered leadership in both words and symbols, offering an alternative view of life and affirming our common humanity across the globe. This same expression has occurred as churches engage with the possibility of war with Iraq and the ethics associated with such actions.

Criticism of church leaders, welfare agency executives, and others who 'meddle' or involve themselves in the formulation of social and economic policy, however, generally only receive the ire of politicians or corporate leaders when they express views or opinions contrary to prevailing politically correct or acceptable viewpoints.

The former Premier of Victoria, Jeff Kennett, regularly criticised churches and church leaders for their engagement in politics, and chastised them for not worrying about empty pews. Academics and corporate leaders regularly challenge the church, accusing them of being ignorant about social and economic agenda. In a similar vein, when leaders of faith-based welfare agencies speak about the social and economic costs of gambling, or the targetting of welfare reform which discriminates against women or single parents, or the treatment of asylum seekers, or the impact of globalisation, they are often reminded by government not to become political and to remember their contractual obligations.

This has been the case recently when church advocates pleaded for a fairer treatment of asylum seekers or for the plight of homeless men and women, or when expressing challenges to globalisation and other social and economic policies which discriminate against or exploit members of the community. As we see in the current debates surrounding a possible war with Iraq, there is often an expectation that the church will bless the moral agenda of the governments.

Christian faith at its best responds to the human condition of suffering when it seeks to give more than comfort and wise platitudes, when it seeks, in the experiences of suffering and joy, to find and name the presence of the divine. Here, in these experiences, we are confronted with the reality of the human being which is able to rise to great heights, while at the same time commit outrageous atrocities against each other. In the experiences of Bali, amidst pain, suffering and death, we have been told of heroic examples of individuals who risked their lives for others, offering hope amidst despair.

Part of the tragedy of human experience has always been our capacity for good and evil, and the knowledge we all have of our own capacity to do both.

Christians, however, often express a one-sided or singular view about salvation, hope and forgiveness, stating that the saving work of God is only personal in intent and has no significant communal intentions. It is not that Christians are unaware that God's love and justice is for all of creation, and that the generosity of the spirit is unconditional. They, however, do often limit this hospitality by dogma and personal prejudice and ideology which binds up rather than liberates the human person. The exercise of communal justice as servant ministry, then, is understood as secondary to evangelism and personal commitment.

The church is often understood as a single entity. The reality is that the church is broad in its beliefs and its core objectives. This reality is often not acknowledged, and in some cases is not seen as 'good copy' for newspapers when they wish to highlight conflict within churches. Like others in the community, the church does not always speak with one voice on social issues. While this may be disconcerting to some, both inside and outside the church, it is an essential life-giving element to a stable democracy.

Writing in his introduction to the recently released report by the Victorian Council of Churches, entitled *The Church and the Free Market*, Brian Howe, former Deputy Prime Minister, Minister for Social Security, and a Uniting Church Minister, says this:

> Whatever conclusions one may come to about Jesus, it is important to understand the context in which he struggled to reinterpret the historic faith of Judaism, while remaining very much within its traditions. We can grasp the shift from essentially a rule-based ethic to a more personalistic ethic based on love . . . God's love was not restricted to those who were free from disease but extended to those whose illness or disease seemed to be the greatest threat to the wellbeing of others. While God's love has been evident in the history of Israel it was in no sense restricted to one race or one people. The

> ethic which Jesus taught was based on the theological perspective which included those that seemed to have been excluded under the old order.
>
> Of course, in challenging this system, Jesus also was destroying the authority of those who had a vested interest in its preservation. This undermining of the power structure would inevitably bring him into sharp conflict with those who were benefiting most from the existence of the purity system. [2]

One outstanding contributor to an Anglican strategy of social responsibility and justice can be seen in the ministry of Bishop Ernest Burgman, Bishop of Goulburn 1934–50, and Bishop of Canberra and Goulburn 1950–60.

In his ministry there is a well-documented activism in the fields of social and economic reform and the pursuit of a just society. Peter Hempenstall, in an article written in 1989 about Burgman, said: 'he had a dream, a dream about a great Christian democracy evolving in Australia, which would give a lead to the rest of the world in consensus, co-operation and social justice'.[3]

Hempenstall goes on to describe Burgman as standing in the great tradition of Anglican social thinkers.[4] Critical inquiry embracing a whole-of-life approach was central to his ministry and in his engagement with others. As Hempenstall further says: 'he saw in present social conditions the continuation of Calvary'.[5] Burgman goes on to say: 'if comfortable clergymen were to escape the guilt of participating in the daily crucifixion of men and women they must actively engage themselves in the process of social reform'.[6] In addition, Burgman wrote letters to the editor, published articles challenging and criticising capitalism as a distorted form of political economy. He tried to rouse the Anglican Church, indeed all churches, in this agenda, and was active in the public arena on many social and

---

2. B Howe and others, *The Church and the Free Marke*t (Adelaide: ATF Press, 2002), 2.
3. P Hempenstall, *'An Anglican Strategy for Social Responsibility'*, published in *Anglican Strategies from Burgman to the Present* (Broughton Press 1989), 2.
4. *Ibid*, 1ff.
5. *Ibid*, 3.
6. *Ibid*, 3.

economic issues. He went out into the open to disturb people's minds and to challenge their presuppositions.

He accused his own church of standing aside during the depression. In 1938 he boldly told his colleagues:

> It is the business of the church to minister to sick and neurotic souls, yet it ends up far too often with these fearful, neurotic souls in the saddle so far as the institution is concerned.
>
> The church has failed to bear witness to international justice, as she has failed to bear witness to justice in inter-class relations. As her failure in the later case produced communism, so her failure in the former has given us Nazism and fascism.
>
> Churches are always a danger to religion, they get interested in themselves, in their own aggrandisement and power and countless things that keep them too busy to live close to the life of the people. Churchmen get interested in the world beyond this world, largely to escape the trouble of setting right the wrongs that afflict the human race.[7]

Reactions to Burgman, Gerard Tucker, Geoffrey Sambell, Peter Hollingworth, David Scott and others, continue to this present day. Those who seek to raise the flag for a more just and compassionate community aligned with the Christian principles of justice and equality are often seen as ill-informed and ignorant.

Christian leaders who stand on the side of the disadvantaged, calling for equity and a just distribution of the nation's commonwealth, are viewed with suspicion, and at best, often seen as good people, yet somewhat mistaken. Feeding the hungry is a noble act, but attacking the causes of hunger is seen as disturbing.

The postmodern world of today claims for itself that it has the potential to shape human destiny, and the historic role of religion and God is no longer relevant.

These claims are made in the midst of the world's current turmoils, and the fact that two-thirds of the world still lives in poverty. The

7. *Ibid*, 5.

richest nations of the world continue to exploit the less powerful and deny the reality of their deeds. At the end of the Second World War, the question was asked, 'How could civilised humanity commit such atrocities?' The question still remains unanswered. Simply to dismiss the contribution of faith, the engagement of church leaders and welfare executives in political debates about the nature of our community and the social and economic issues confronting our world, when such a question remains unanswered, is simplistic. To blame religion for all acts of terrorism ignores the place humanity itself plays in creating such actions.

Christians affirm that, in the person of Jesus, we witness and experience the face of God, and see in his life the outpouring of love for all of humankind. In Jesus we see what God expects of us. Peter, the close friend, follower and disciple of Jesus, portrays both sides of the human condition. Peter desires to do the best and the right thing, but when put to the test, fails, his desire to be faithful held back by his own vulnerability and weakness. This is a popular story because it reflects the life of so many of us. Our capacity for good is so often weakened by ourselves.

The story of Peter and of his relationship with Jesus tells of the nature of God's generosity. Jesus still accepts Peter despite his failure to live up to expectations.

Modern science has helped to explain many aspects of our humanity previously understood by myth and story. Today, psychology, along with other of the social sciences, helps us in interpreting and understanding our actions, but does not dispel the reality that as creatures we are still struggling with our capacity for good and evil.

Christians affirm that in Jesus of Nazareth we gain insights into the call to be holy, compassionate and just in our dealings with our fellows and all of the created order. He demonstrates the capacity for forgiveness, while pointing to a way forward as a means of reaching our fulfilment. In the story of the prodigal son, this message is told with remarkable clarity and insight. Perhaps one reason why numbers of people in the West are resisting the Christian faith is because of the heavy expectation on all of us to examine our own lives in the face of increasing suffering and pain and to be ready to forgive when the facts suggest otherwise.

Perhaps the challenge facing the Christian faith in its engagement with society is the threat that society may feel that a revitalised faith will challenge its own social agenda and self-indulgence.

The circumstances of the younger son's request in the story of the prodigal son suggest behaviour towards the father which many of us would find insulting and arrogant. The son would not wait for his inheritance, he wanted it now.

The father, we are told, obliges and the son goes on a spending spree and loses all. Then, when faced with destitution, the son returns as an outcast and confesses his failures, not asking for his previous place in the family, but hoping for a job as a farmhand. The father has a different response. Without waiting for a confession, he races towards his son so that the son can be spared the wrath and anger of others, and the father takes upon himself the initiative to invite his son back into the household. The father embraces the son, putting his own hurts and shame to the side.

This outrageous love and never-ending heartache of God is at the centre of the good news of the Christian faith. This claim is extraordinary in a world at war with itself. It is a way of acknowledging and responding to the hurts of our times and provides a framework and ethic for our relationships with one another across cultures and faiths. It requires not only a change of heart from those who break promises, commit crimes and exploit others, but also from those who are victims. Those of us who try to live this way often fail as we ourselves grapple with life and death issues. Moral judgments and pronouncements when they occur are normally less than helpful. What are helpful are words of hope and forgiveness. They demonstrate a willingness to engage in dialogue and seek solutions that are just and forgiving.

A distinctive Christian understanding of creation embodies a belief in our common humanity, communion in its fullest sense. It calls for a naming of the divine in our midst and the recognition of Christ in the least of our brothers and sisters. Structures and policy which diminish the human person, marginalise and exploit, should be challenged.

Building a just community is not the same as managing or psychologising the poor. Instead, a just community is about rights, relationships and responsibilities. It is about the creation of the kingdom of God here in this place at this time.

The church and its leaders cannot afford not to engage in the politics of civil life. Not that church leaders will always get it right. We can be tempted by a messiah complex and believe that we have the only answer. In our engagement with civil society, the approach needs to be one of both dialogue and moral persuasion. When rebuked by politicians and corporate leaders, this may often suggest that the church has something to say, however distasteful, and at times less than persuasive.

Christians have a perspective of life and in a democratic society we have the responsibility and privilege to be a contributor to the debates on issues which shape our world. A healthy democracy requires a robust and passionate engagement with both individuals and groups who make up the society. The church's role is to engage in the debates on all issues which shape our common humanity. To do otherwise diminishes the freedom Christ seeks to offer all, rich and poor.

The Foreign Minister, Alexander Downer, recently voiced his concern at the manner in which members of the church participate in political debate. He was concerned at what he described as clerics who seek 'cheap headlines' and are:

> remarkably vague and uncertain about matters which their faith should teach them with certitude but remarkably certain and dogmatic on matters of considerable complexity and ambiguity about which they have no practical expertise.[8]

The sentiment is not new and his words echo those of other politicians before him. The once Prime Minister of England, Margaret Thatcher, expressed her irritation at British prelates who opposed her economic rationalism. Mr Downer's suggestion is that the church should stop involving itself with 'partisan politicking' and concentrate on the spiritual and moral issues.

But as Archbishop Mannix observed, politicians like to complain about interfering clerics when they are on opposing sides.

Today, many Western governments call on religion when it suits them to justify their view of world order, and are infuriated when religion, particularly, the mainstream Christian faiths, raises challenges to such exploitation and false interpretation of faith.

It is in fact a responsibility of the church to speak out against those who 'turn justice to wormwood, and bring righteousness to the

---

8. The full text of the Alexander Downer's 'Playford Lecture' is included in this volume, pages 13–20.

ground!' (Amos 5:7). To concentrate on spiritual and moral issues demands that the church becomes involved in political debate.

The truth is that the Christian church, along with other religious groups, is well placed to participate in the dialogue between community and policy makers when it comes to issues of social justice, welfare and ethical concern.

Religion, when it is not abused by false and misleading prophets, or is dogmatic on ethical and justice issues, has the potential to be a major influence for good. True religious expression is when it liberates humanity from its own self-centredness and gives each of us an ethic of compassion for the whole of creation.

The church is called to offer a lived example, but is not constrained from participating in open and constructive dialogue, to ask questions, to consider issues and to hold opinions guided by the moral and ethical foundations of faith.

Religion is concerned with the wellbeing of all creation, both human and environmental.

It seeks to share the bounty of the earth fairly, distribute its resources wisely and encourage and protect the values of justice, compassion, mercy and inclusiveness. These are the standards upon which our social order is based and our political system is charged to defend.

In this society it means that clerics and laypeople of all religions need to participate in the political process, as it is the structure within which the mechanics of the stewardship of the whole earth and humanity resides.

Participation takes many forms: living example, dialogue, education. To truly live out the Christian ethic the church must act within the community. The church must participate in the whole process, including having a political voice.

The Church and Civil Society: Mutual Obligation

John Pettman

1. Mutual obligation versus shared responsibility

In John Bell's and Graham Maule's Iona Community song 'Inspired by Love and Anger' the first verse reads:

> Inspired by love and anger,
> Disturbed by need and pain,
> Informed of God's own bias,
> We ask him once again:
> 'How long must some folk suffer?
> How long can few folk mind?
> How long dare vain self-interest
> Turn prayer and pity blind?'

When I first heard this song I too was stirred by love and anger. Love for the powerless, the exploited, the hurting; and anger, gut-wrenching anger, about a community that lets individuals and families suffer on and on, from one generation to the next. There is a growing gap between the rich and the poor, between those who can fend for themselves and those who cannot. In my community I see kids who are caught in a downward poverty spiral from which there is little hope of escape. Their families have little money, no employment, poor food and nutrition with the consequent health problems, lack of motivation and indifference to education. It is a trap, which leads to despair and no contemplated future. Blaming the individuals is not the answer; we have an obligation, as Christians, to enable them to escape this poverty trap.

2. Obligation

Obligation in a church-based community service organisation, whether mutual or otherwise, arises out of the twofold covenant we have with God. It is twofold because our obligations are firstly to God and secondly to others or our neighbours.

To what extent then can we accept, within the community service setting, the concept of mutual obligation? As Dorothy McRae-Mc Mahon points out in her article in *Civilising Community for Us All*. 'The concept of mutual obligation is relatively meaningless until it is further defined', and asks, ' Is it simply that those who receive money from the state (the sum total of the state's obligation) have an obligation to earn and deserve that money?'[1]

The question is how far can we as Christian community service agencies go along with an understanding of mutual obligation that states that all who receive help ought to earn it or meet some other criteria that says they deserve help. I do not know how the government defines 'deserve'.

A young woman who lives near me had never had regular employment in her life. Except for a training program, she had received the dole since reaching the appropriate age. She desperately wanted to work, so work for the dole was a very attractive concept for her. To be wanted, to do something, even required to do something, work filling her days and lifting herself esteem. She was given work. It was an hour's travel from her home, there was no transport in the morning and her pensioner father had to drive her to work each morning. The mutual obligation had worked. She had embraced the concept of responsibility, the government department had found work for her and she received the dole. But such an arrangement is unacceptable to us because it is unjust and it was subsidised by her father providing the cost of travel to employment.

3. A living wage

There is no doubt that the Christian gospel provides a motif related to work and the willingness to work. In Matthew 20 we have the story

---

1. 'Mutual Obligation', in *Civilising Community for Us All* (Adelaide: ATF Press, 2000), 63.

which Jesus tells regarding a vineyard operator who sought workers in the marketplace (or employment agency).

There are a number of aspects of this story that are worth evaluating. First there was a desperate need for labour. Without it the grape crop could spoil. So we start from a premise of self-interest of the employer, and that is not bad. It is the basis of most commerce. Secondly, he goes to the marketplace a number of times during the day to enlist more labour, his motivation is still to harvest the crop. On the last visit, at five o'clock, still looking for more workers, he encounters people standing around and says to them. 'Why are you standing around idle all day?' There is an implied judgment here. If they had been looking for work they would have been there earlier. It would have been possible for them to ascertain where work was being offered in the district, the comings and goings in the marketplace would not have been unnoticed. Having rebuked the workers and I am afraid still motivated by self-interest, he sends them to work. But now there is a dramatic change in the story. Irrespective of the number of hours worked, all were paid a living wage, recognition of the needs of the person and their family. There is no doubt that the employer saw an obligation that people had to work and look for work. On the other hand, the employer accepted his obligation to provide a living wage for the workers. Of course, those who had worked longer hours and were paid the same amount were dissatisfied. They had missed the notion of mutual obligation to their fellow workers.

4. Grace and forgiveness

For the Christian community service organisation, responsibility goes hand in hand with grace. Grace that can be defined as underserved favour. It is grace that God gives to us, and it is grace which we are obliged to give to others. The government policy of mutual obligation does not allow for forgiveness. It is in the story of the prodigal son that we encounter a picture of the unconditional love of God. Here is a person who takes from his father that which would not by rights be his until his father's death. Having behaved in such an audacious way, he then wastes the money, which should have provided for him in the years to come. There is no evidence of responsibility here, no accountability and no demonstrated skill, and yet when all else fails he returns home to enjoy the father's generosity and forgiveness. This is how the church is called upon to demonstrate its obligations by being forgiving to those who for one reason or another have wasted what they have. The church acts responsibly in obedience to the gospel, forgives and assists those who have not been responsible. The gospel does not allow us to reject the wasteful or the neglectful; however, part of our responsibility is to judge carefully what help, support and encouragement needs to be given to all persons. The church community service agencies must also be accountable to their stakeholders, those providing money, government and otherwise, as to how it meets its obligation to those in need.

5. Accountability

Accountability for the expenditure of funds is an ethical must of this day and age. However, church community groups applying for government funds must make it quite clear as to the principles behind their administration of those funds. To accept funds and use them in a way that is not in keeping with government policy is dishonest, and we must either convince the government of the validity of our program or refuse funds.

Accountability is to all stakeholders. This may include government, but it must also include the church and the wider community. The community itself has a good grasp of what is just and fair, and it also has a grasp of what is responsible. It is very hard for the community to accept that some executives should be paid millions of dollars and others are reduced to eating pet food. Those who have wealth also need to be brought into the 'mutual obligation' equation. Where the choice is to install new plant and reduce the workforce, account needs to be taken of those left unemployed and families that are impoverished in the cause of greater profits. The prophet Amos, active centuries ago, noted that the righteous were sold for silver and the needy for a pair of sandals. Amos spoke out against the misuse of power in his day. Unfortunately, market forces always seem to work against the powerless, and humans are categorised as resources or production units. Industry and organisations, including the church, need to take seriously their responsibility to their employees as well as to their shareholders. It is the growing rift between the rich and poor that needs to be taken up by government when its looks at the economic management of the nation. Tim Costello reminds us of the ideals of a previous Australian government in his book *Tips from a Travelling Soul-searcher* when he quotes Curtin and Chifley:

> Government is first and foremost a moral contract, not an economic contract. If you give us your best citizenship to rebuild communities in this nation, make the sacrifices necessary, we promise to listen to you, to respond to your needs, and invite you to participate in this enterprise called democracy.

We need to challenge the rift between moral responsibility and economic management.

6. Respect

There is a wonderful story in the book of Acts. It concerns the disciples Peter and John and a lame person that they met at the temple gate called Beautiful. Here was a man crippled since birth. A man who had begged for sustenance all his life. Not only did he have to put up with his frail physical condition, but also the judgment of the culture which held that the disabled had somehow or other offended God and this was their punishment. Here was a man oppressed by illness and culture. The disciples looked at him intently and said to him, 'Look at us'. In other words, do not be down cast but look up. If you have had experience of people begging in the street you will often notice that the eyes are downcast, shame seems to stop them relating. Peter and John broke through this shame and feeling of inferiority. They treated this man with dignity; they showed respect for him as a person. I remember speaking with a young woman who had been on the free list at school. Her family were registered as poor and could not provide even a pencil. She told me of how she would cringe when in class the teacher administered charity. She was different, not a real person, she was one of those free list people, the ones who did not count. I do not particularly like the term clients or customers for those who are in relationship with our agencies, but the word customer does in fact promote a concept of respect of which we should take note. Government policy also ought to show respect for those who are recipients of care.

7. Release for the captives

The mission of Jesus included release for the captives, particularly those who were unfairly captive in the culture of the day. His acceptance and help extending to the woman with a haemorrhage, the leper branded unclean, the tax collector accused of being an exploiter, the blind man beside the road and that man seized with evil fits. All of these were held captive, and Jesus moved to release them. Christian community services move towards people who are held captive and are powerless in our society. They moved towards those who are captive of poverty, poor housing, drugs, mental illness, physical disabilities, sexual abuse, racial discrimination and sexual prejudice and many others. As community service organisation we do it as best we can with limited funds and resources. We do it on behalf of the community as they provide funds through the government as a part of their mutual obligation. However, we cannot differentiate between those who deserve help and those who do not. Action must be taken to improve persons' and families' quality of life and images of self-worth. Those who are captured and held prisoner by their current circumstances need to be released, and as a total community we have a responsibility to do just that.

However, while we hold to a tenet of care for all, we also hold that care must be individual and appropriate. With some it will be harm minimisation, with others it will be skill training or employment or food or housing or medical help. A part of our responsibility is to provide care after careful assessment and a diligent use of funds. A part of that assessment may be mapping the past experience of a person and helping them to accept responsibility for the past. Sometimes assessment can help discern valuable lessons in the past experience that can be used in the future and a sense a self-responsibility encouraged to grow. During this process of assessment, learning and growth, social security sanctions are not appropriate. Why? Because the mutual obligation surrounding this person and their family includes church, government, community and employers. Do we sanction government when it makes a mistake? Or a community when it rejects a black family? Or an employer when it sacks people? Rather, all should share the opportunity to enhance the lives of others.

8. Scope

We fall short of our obligations when care is reduced to basics like work for the dole or bed and board for the elderly. In an aged-care unit there are many needs beyond the bed and board and medical necessities. An elderly person entering a hostel or a nursing home has a number of emotional and spiritual problems to deal with, and good care will recognise these needs. They included isolation, grief related to losing existing home, perhaps loss of a loved one and most certainly loss of many precious possessions. There are problems coping with failing memory and physical ability and accepting limitations. There are questions about death and sometimes fear of death. All of these cannot be wrapped up in simple cash payment for bed and board.

There is a danger that we can, as a society or government, treat those in need as a problem rather than as a member of our community. Those for whom we care are not only individuals but also members of a network of important relationships. Those relationships may include mother, father, siblings, partner, spouse, children and close friends. It is wrong to separate care from the environment in which a person lives, because that environment may indeed be the key to their support. By blaming the poor for their own plight we also condemn their partner, wife, children, family to suffer alongside them. Careful assessment does not reduce care to just an individual injection of funds.

9. Shared responsibility

There is a biblical motif about sharing the responsibility for those in need. It is found in the book of Acts and is that section where deacons were appointed by the early church to care for widows and orphans. A number were chosen to undertake this task, which left the disciples free to carry out other responsibilities. Here there are three groups exercising responsibility. Firstly, the whole church community who sees the need for specialist action. Secondly, the disciples who rightly recognise that they cannot do everything and are willing to enlist others to help. The third group are those chosen and entrusted with the task.

This pattern needs to be replicated in today's society at a secular level. The community at large must bear responsibility for those who are disadvantaged, in need and powerless. However, they are not able to effect the specialised help that is required and must fund their requirements through government. The government must choose whether to do the task themselves through their own agencies or seek the help of other specialists to put into effect carefully planned programs.

Care must not be reduced to the action of a few 'goody-goody' groups. The needs of people in our community today are complex and difficult to deal with. Community service organisations need to employ specialists who are trained and skilled in a number of various fields. This needs to be coupled with motivation and compassion so as to bring meaningful life to others.

Everald Compton, writing in the *National Seniors* magazine of June 2001, stated:

> However, the heart of the matter is this. No matter how good or bad politicians may be they cannot legislate to turn us into the caring and sharing society we should be. No laws can force us to be friendly, generous, helpful and concerned. We must change society for the better at the grass roots level.

No laws can force us to be friends, generous, helpful, concerned or responsible. The current concept of mutual obligation is one of coercion and compulsion. This does not promote responsibility but rather resentment. A better approach is for the community as a whole to be responsible for its citizens and enable the powerless to become strong, the unemployed to gain work, the unskilled to be trained and those caught in the poverty trap to be set free.

Community service organisations have a responsibility to inform and persuade both the grass roots of our society along with government and business leaders, so that our community can be democratic and just for all. This will happen more readily if responsibility is shared across society.

Part IV

Theological Perspectives

Spirituality and Trauma

Geoff Schirmer

I present a compressed and personal account of spirituality and trauma. Hopefully, along the way, there are points that connect with the spirit of this conference.

In essence, my spirituality, my journey of faith, is grounded in taking time to be still with God, and in the stillness to be touched and shaped by the mystery of the presence of Christ—the One who lives in us, and we in him.

At the same time, this process, this way of being, is inevitably contextual. It is grounded in the current circumstances of my journey.

During the past seven years, as a hospital chaplain, my context has been one in which I am regularly in contact with suffering and death, as well as recovery and wellbeing.

Four years ago my wife became mentally ill, an illness caused by unresolved trauma related to abuse inflicted on her by her father when she was fourteen. Actually, abuse is too cosmetic a word. The reality is that she was beaten and raped by her father in a series of attacks which became progressively more violent. Our context is one in which we are caught up in the traumatic process of working on the impact which this abuse continues to have on our marriage, and on our children.

1. A spirituality of 'the theology of the cross': a spirituality of paradox

In the stillness—in Christ—I am led to reflect upon, and struggle with, my life situation in the light of the theology of the cross. Here I have in mind Luther's theology of the cross, in which he not only saw the cross in terms of the atoning sacrifice of Christ, but also as the paradigm for the manner in which God is present in our lives, and at work in our lives, in Christ.

As a hospital chaplain, my spirituality, my reflection is grounded in:

- an awareness that each encounter with a patient is an encounter with Christ

- an awareness that through encounters with the cross of the patient, and with my own cross, Christ is shaping me to be his servant

- the paradox that 'in, with, and under'[1] weakness, vulnerability, and suffering, both of the patient and myself, Christ is present with his grace.

In relation to my wife and my family, my spirituality, my struggle revolves around:

- the paradox that 'in, with, and under' this most grievous *anfechtung* (Tillich's 'attacks of utter despair'[2]) this abuse which stirs within me such a feral desire for justice, which has deprived us of so much, which I so much despise, and from which I am convinced nothing good can come—'in, with, and under' this most unlikely source, Christ has mercy, strength, and life for my wife, for our family, and for myself.

To put it another way, my spiritual struggle revolves around the question: 'What did Christ have in mind for me when he led me to fall in love with a woman who had been beaten and raped by her father?'

In my wrestling I am sustained by Walther von Loewenich in his commentary on Thesis 20 of Luther's Heidelberg Disputation:

> 'Cross' and 'suffering' refer, in the first place, to Christ's suffering and cross. But Luther is thinking at the same time about the cross of the Christian. For Luther the cross of Christ and the cross of the Christian belong together . . . The essence of the ultimate character of reality has become clear at this point. There is no honest communion with God that tries to go behind this evidence (cf Thesis 21). This

---

1. A phrase used by Martin Luther to express the mystery of the sacramental presence and grace of Christ.
2. Paul Tillich, *The Courage to Be* (London: Fontana, 1965), 165.

> evidence, however, cannot be grasped by pure contemplation. Precisely because the total character of reality has become evident here, a decision concerning my existence has been made. Thus if I want to acknowledge this evidence seriously, I must affirm it with my whole existence. That is to say, the cross of the Christian corresponds to the cross of Christ. To know God 'through suffering and the cross' means that the knowledge of God comes into being at the cross of Christ, the significance of which becomes evident only to one who himself stands in cross and suffering.[3]

Alister McGrath sustains the paradox, and the scandal, of the theology of the cross:

> Far from regarding suffering and evil as a nonsensical intrusion into the world (which Luther regards as the opinion of a theologian of glory) the theologian of the cross regards such suffering as his most precious treasure, for revealed and yet hidden in precisely such sufferings is none other than the living God, working out the salvation of those he loves.[4]

2. A spirituality of pathos

There is a deepening awareness of the implications of the in-dwelling presence of Christ—the One who lives in us, and we in him—the One who is nearer to us than our thoughts, closer to us than our next heart-beat—the One in whom we live and move and have our being—the One whose relationship with us is grounded in the covenant: 'I am with you always'.

In particular, an awareness that, in Christ, we are partners in a communion of pathos:

---

3. Walter von Loewenich, *Luther's Theology of the Cross* (Augsburg Press, 1982), 20.

4. Alister McGrath, *Luther's Theology of the Cross* (Oxford: Blackwell, 1985), 151.

- that whatever we suffer, we do not suffer alone—for God, in Christ, is afflicted with us in all our affliction (Isaiah 63:9)

- that 'in, with, and under' our sufferings we are being caught up, together with St Paul, in the mystery that in our flesh we are completing what is lacking in Christ's afflictions for the sake of his body, that is, the church (Col 1:24).

3. A spirituality of lament

Along the way I have also been sustained by the peculiar catharsis of lament. At some of the worst times there has been a sense of sanctuary in the words of Psalm 44:19—'But you have crushed [me] and made [me] a haunt for jackals and covered [me] over with deep darkness'. These words have become flesh for me; they have been loyal companions, and steadfast advocates; they have helped me to utter that which is beyond words.

At the same time this lament has led to another awareness. Since God, in Christ, suffers with us, it follows that God, in Christ, laments with us.

In my experience of grief and lament over what has taken place, there is a part of me that continues to weep inwardly over the appalling violation exacted upon a tender fourteen year old girl at the threshold of womanhood, and at the subsequent destruction visited upon our marriage and upon our children.

If God, in Christ, weeps with me in my weeping, and laments with me in my lamenting—how much more does God have cause to weep and lament over the violation and subsequent destruction to which the entirety of creation has been subjected? To whom can God lament? Ultimately, what does it cost God to be God?

4. The *perichoretic* adagio

John of Damascus (d 749) used the term *perichoresis* to express the mystery of the Trinitarian relationship between the Father and the Son and the Holy Spirit. Catherine LaCugna favours the case for considering *perichoresis* in terms of 'the divine dance'.[5]

In moments of reflection it has seemed appropriate to consider this *perichoresis*, this 'divine dance', as taking the form of a divine adagio.

---

5. Catherine LaCugna, *God for Us: The Trinity in Christian Life* (San Francisco: Harper, 1993), 217.

Through the ages musicians have been moved to embrace the adagio as a means to give expression to the sweet, the sad, the melancholy of the human condition—the human pathos which, in Christ, in *perichoresis*, is the pathos of the Trinity.

The music of the adagio has been, for me, a servant of the spirituality of pathos and lament. The adagio, in Samuel Barber's string quartet, in Mahler's fifth symphony, in Schubert's quintet for strings, as well as any adagio of choice in the sublime works of Bach, to name a few.

In pathos, in Christ, we are caught up in the *perichoretic* adagio—the sweet, sad, pathos of the Trinity—until all things are made new.

'We go to God when he is sorely placed, find him poor, scorned, unsheltered, without bread, whelmed under weight of evil, weak or dead. Christians stand by God in his hour of grief.'[6]

In this it is in Christ, God is caught up in our struggle, our lament, our pathos, as we strive for justice and compassion in a civil society.

---

6. Dietrich Bonhoeffer, *Letters and Papers from Prison* (London: Fontana, 1966), 174; *Australian Lutheran Hymnal with Supplement*, Hymn 780, verse 2.

Faith-based Realities

Harry Herbert

Today I want to look at the issue of why the Christian church is engaged in social and political action. Too often this activity is seen as an intrusion into the normal life of the church, an intrusion of the secular into the sacred. Although, to some extent, we have become used to the intervention of the church in political life in Australia, there are still many who think that it is illegitimate. They see the life of the church as having been disturbed and interrupted by social and political action. I want to argue that this is not the case, and that the church's engagement with the political scene arises from the fundamentals of the faith. Also, I think that when we keep our social and political engagement close to the foundations of the faith it is more likely to be carried out with integrity.

Nevertheless, it is always important to acknowledge that not all political activity carried out by churches over the years has been right and proper. The Germany Christian Movement, organised by the Nazis in Germany in the 1930s, is an example. In this country the role played by the Catholic Church in the development of the Democratic Labor Party and its involvement in the Movement is another. And there are lots of other examples, some of which are related to the church seeking to shore up its own privileged position in Western society or supporting totalitarian regimes in other societies. So, I certainly do not want to imply that all political engagement by the church is good per se. It always needs critical analysis, and I hope by outlining some of the reasons why I think the church should be involved, I am at the same time providing criteria for that analysis.

So, I want to look at these faith foundations, and then go on to look at the second important basis of church engagement with social and political structures, namely, the church's substantial role in the delivery of community services.

In regard to the first I do not want to cover all of the ground, but I do want to give some examples.

Let us take the example of the Christian understanding about forgiveness. In many ways, it differentiates the Christian community from most others in the society. Or, at least it should. Christians believe that because they themselves benefit from the forgiveness of God, they should respond by showing forgiveness to others. Of course, Christians understand that forgiveness has to be balanced with judgment. In the 1988 Ecumenical Report 'Prison: The Last Resort', it is stated that: 'Crime is part of the disorder of the fallen world. If allowed to go unchecked it would make life intolerable for all and result in far greater evil and injury than is the case at present'.[1] That report acknowledges that 'one of the legitimate functions of government is to administer the sanctions a society adopts to ensure laws are upheld'. However, having said that, the Christian understanding of forgiveness does mean that the church must advocate strongly for rehabilitation in prisons, and against harsh and unreasonable punishment. In some parts of Australia, especially in NSW, state election campaigns are correctly described as 'law and order auctions' where each political side attempts to outdo the other in proposing harsher laws and punishments. Becoming involved in comment or criticism about the criminal justice system is inevitably a political act. To introduce the theme of forgiveness into the discussion is bound to be met with scorn and derision from most political parties. And yet, challenging the community to change its attitudes to imprisonment, retaining rehabilitation as an important feature of prisons, and arguing against unreasonably lengthy sentences or unreasonable restrictions on bail, could all be said to legitimately arise from the Christian belief in forgiveness.

Repentance is another foundation of the Christian faith. Christians believe that it is important that we are willing to say 'sorry' when we have done wrong in order to receive God's forgiveness. Again, this is not a popular concept in the public arena. Often, along with forgiveness, it is seen to be more akin to weakness rather than strength. The general rule of political life is to never admit a mistake. To do so is seen as a sign of failure. In the Human Rights and Equal Opportunity Commission Report, *Bringing Them Home*,[2] which examined the

---

1. *Prison: The Last Resort* (Melbourne: Collins Dove, 1988), 31.
2. *Bringing Them Home* (Sydney: Human Rights and Equal Opportunities Commission, 1997).

separation of Aboriginal and Torres Strait Islander children from their families, one of the recommendations was that there be acknowledgments and apologies from all Australian parliaments, churches, and other non-government organisations which had played a role in the policies of forcible removal of Indigenous children from their parents. Considerable controversy followed the release of the report. The Australian Prime Minister, John Howard, has consistently refused to participate in making an apology, although many parliaments, churches, and non-government groups have done so. To enter this debate is inevitably political. It could not be otherwise. However, surely there is a powerful argument that says that our Christian understanding of repentance lays an obligation on us to enter that debate and to advocate the importance of repentance in national life as a way forward.

Surely no one would doubt the importance of care and compassion in the Christian faith. The love of God is a continual theme in the faith. Indeed, it is the pre-eminent theme of the faith. The Christian scriptures are replete with stories which emphasise the love of God. Jesus of Nazareth was the incarnation of God and he reached out to the weak and poor, the marginalised, the sick, and the outsiders. In Jesus' parables, such as the good samaritan or the final judgment, and in his teachings, there is a clear emphasis on love of neighbour. Throughout the whole history of the church we can see how that fundamental belief has been central to its life. And yet, again, we must acknowledge that to fulfil this teaching in our own day will inevitably involve us in political and social action.

In his book, *Borderline*, which is about Australia's treatment of refugees and asylum seekers, Peter Mares comments on the important role which the Christian community has played in supporting asylum seekers and in advocating for their rights. Having written about one program in Melbourne where a church worker helped asylum seekers get free medical attention and prescription drugs, Mares writes:

> Such acts of generosity are testament to the well of sympathy for asylum seekers that does exist in the community. It is also a powerful reminder of the role of the churches in maintaining a sense of conscience and public responsibility in Australia. Time and again it is churchgoers or clergy who step in to provide support for asylum seekers or refugees

> —whether it is through pastoral visits to detention centres, advocacy, accommodation services, or tins of food.[3]

His reference to 'pastoral visits' reminds us that pastoral care, which is usually viewed as essentially individualistic and generally regarded as a benign religious function, itself becomes political when it is put in the context of detention centres and the overall policy on asylum seekers. In another part of his excellent book, Peter Mares gives the account of the difficulties of both the Uniting Church minister and the Catholic priest to conduct services of worship at Woomera Detention Centre, again indicating that even the conduct of worship can at times become controversial and political.

And yet, despite the appearance of solely political action, it can be easily seen that the activity of the churches and Christian people in regard to the unjust asylum seeker policies in Australia are no more than a practical expression of the Christian commandment to 'love one's neighbour', and the biblical injunction to visit those in prison. Again, in a similar vein, the Declaration of Religious Leaders, issued early in 2003, concerning the return of asylum seekers to their countries of origin where their lives were in danger, is a political action, but it results from a Christian understanding of care and compassion.

Opposing discrimination against minority groups can be easily portrayed as political, when, again, it also arises from the Christian faith's core belief in love of neighbour. Support of the rights of gay people, religious minorities, and others may lead to action which is at first viewed as political. However, on closer analysis it can be seen to flow directly from some of the most basic tenets of the Christian faith.

I hope that I am beginning to show with these examples that social and political engagement is not an option for the Christian church. In my view it is integral to the life of faith. I could have chosen lots of other examples, such as the Jubilee Campaign to address Third World debt. This is a clearly political campaign, but arises directly from the Christian understanding about humanity and the equality of people before God. My overall message is that what appears at first sight to be

---

3. Peter Mares, *Borderline* (Sydney: UNSW Press, 2001), 93.

political can soon be seen to be nothing more than the practical application of Christian values and beliefs.

The second area where we see why the church is drawn into engagement with social and political forces in the society is the church's role in the provision of community services. For historical and other reasons, the Christian churches in Australia are among the largest non-government organisations delivering community services to Australian citizens. In the 1995 report of the Industry Commission [now the Productivity Commission] into Charitable Organisations in Australia, twenty of the fifty largest groups were church organisations, and many others were indirectly linked to churches or had a religious basis.[4] As government policy changes and governments are increasingly taking themselves out of direct service delivery of community services, the involvement of churches is increasing. It is a frequently commented-upon irony that at the same time as churches decline in membership as worshipping communities, their role in community services is rapidly expanding. Since the report of the Industry Commission we have seen the tendering out of the 'Jobs Network' program by the commonwealth government and that, all by itself, has led to a massive expansion of some groups, such as the Salvation Army.

Churches generally accept that they cannot undertake this role within the society and not have it linked to political and social advocacy. This seems less so for the Salvation Army, for instance, but for the Catholic, Anglican, and Uniting Churches it is a core understanding. Those three churches, for instance, are very large providers of services to people needing aged care, either residential or community based. When the Howard Coalition Government proposed the introduction of accommodation bonds for nursing home residents, all three churches indicated their opposition and linked with other organisations, including consumer groups, to force the government to back down, which it eventually did. There is no doubt that the introduction of accommodation bonds for nursing homes would have given a significant financial boost to those church operators. Their opposition, in other words, was not based on self-interest, but on their perception of the overall needs of aged people in Australia. They feared a two-tiered system of nursing homes, where operators in high

4. *Charitable Organisations in Australia*, Industry Commission Report number 45, 16 June 1995 (Melbourne: Australian Government Publishing Service).

income areas could provide a very high standard and expect very high accommodation bonds, while in lower income areas standards would fall because the ability to raise large bonds would be restricted. I give that example because it shows that church aged-care operators do view these issues from a broader perspective and do look at them from the perspective of aged people generally and not just their own clients and residents.

Again, if we take the example of disability services, it would be impossible for the church to be engaged in that area of work and not find itself drawn into political action. In disability, as in most areas of community services, the needs far outweigh the resources applied to meet them. If nothing else, the role of the church is to continually draw attention to the unmet needs and to exhort both the community and governments to do something to address it. While it is reasonable for government, for its part, to press church agencies to work more efficiently and to use the resources they are given to best advantage, it will remain the case that resources are not sufficient to meet the needs. This is particularly so in the case of disability services. A small coalition in Sydney has been working over recent years to get action from the NSW Government to address the needs of disadvantaged people with disabilities who live in privately operated boarding houses. The coalition includes a number of church welfare groups. Their work has inevitably led to political action, and to some extent has been successful. However, it would be naïve and wrong for any church to be working in an area such as this and simply to accept the status quo when there is an obvious and glaring need for change.

My point here is that there can be no escape from social and political engagement once the church has accepted its role as a service provider. Otherwise, the church will become nothing more than a sub-contractor for government services and will be indistinguishable from private operators. It should be a fundamental feature of the church's provision of community services that it is accompanied by advocacy and lobbying on behalf of both the direct users and potential users.

I turn briefly to some practical aspects of this political action. I think it is a mistake to think that churches only engage in political action by making statements or declarations. These have an important part to play but are far from the whole story. Informal and behind-the-scenes lobbying can be just as significant. But, in both cases it needs to be well informed and well reasoned. While the motivation of the church will always arise from its faith and belief, it must be cast in such a way as to engage wider community support. In his statement for the New Millennium, Pope John Paul II wrote:

> For Christian witness to be effective it is important that special efforts be made to explain properly the reasons for the Church's position, stressing that it is not a case of imposing on non-believers a vision based on faith, but of interpreting and defending the values rooted in the very nature of the human person.[5]

I think that is very important, and I would argue that the language the church needs to use is the language of human rights which can be understood in the broader community. It is not a matter of abandoning our faith but of our using language which is more broadly understood.

There are two other important aspects of how we should go about this work. Firstly, we should work together as churches as much as possible. It is not only more effective for this work to be undertaken ecumenically where possible, but it is a more appropriate witness to the gospel. Secondly, we should be willing to work in broader coalitions with community groups, consumer organisations, and, where appropriate, trade unions.

On the issue of research and fact-finding, I think there are two sides of the coin. On the one hand, we need to be clear about what we are seeking in the way of change and political action, and good research is always valuable. On the other hand, we need to recognise our limitation in this regard and not use the lack of complete solutions and information as an excuse for inaction. The amount of information available to the church on complex issues such as tax reform, globalisation, environmental issues and the economy will always be limited. Take economic issues as a case in point. Whatever information about the economy can be put together by the church will always seem puny in relation to the vast resources of the government in this area. However, it does not take a full-scale analysis to identify basic inequities and flaws in an economic program. Indeed, the church can perform a valuable role in concentrating on its own area of expertise,

---

5. Apostolic Letter of Pope John Paul II (Sydney: St Pauls Publications, 2001), 68.

which is moral analysis. In other words, looking at current government policies from the perspective of fairness and justice. When the tax reform package was announced by the government, prior to the introduction of the Goods and Services Tax (GST), church welfare groups, despite what is sometimes now said, were not opposed to the GST per se. However, they did oppose the shift from direct to indirect taxation because they saw it as unfair to low-income groups, and they also opposed some aspects of the so-called compensation package because they thought it was inadequate. They could do this without having the enormous resources of the Australian treasury at their disposal because they were arguing from a moral, rather than an economic, perspective.

Now that churches are large providers of community services, and some of those services such as aged care and 'Jobs Network' have the potential to generate surpluses, they must be prepared to devote some of those resources to boosting their activities in lobbying and advocacy.

Of course, just as the reasons for the church's engagement with political structures arise, in my view, from the fundamentals of the faith, I would also argue that the way in which we engage must also be consistent with our faith fundamentals. In other words, we ought to be honest and act with integrity. We should rise about personality politics and concentrate on the policy issues and avoid exaggerated or pseudo-emotional approaches.

There is no doubt for me that the church's own beliefs and its role in Australian society give it no option but to engage with social and political systems and structures, and it should do so vigorously, persistently, and with integrity.

Resonance and Dissonance between Church and Society

Stephen Ames

1. Introduction

In the light of the gospel of Christ, how should we understand and act on the *dissonances* and the *resonances* between the church and our society? This is my theme.

The orientation of the paper is summed up in the view that the mission of the church is to bear witness to the kind of world this is. This witness is not just in the terms with which the world bears testimony to itself, but also and especially in terms of the kind of God revealed in Christ. The task is to draw out the *dissonances* and *resonances* between these two testimonies and how we should act on them.

All reflections are from some 'position', and since I am a priest in the Anglican Diocese of Melbourne, I will be drawing on my experience of this church, which is the one I know best. I trust my brothers and sisters in Christ will make their own connections to and critiques of the churches they know best. Here is something of my image of the Anglican Church in Melbourne.

a. The indicators of the overall life the church in the diocese show that we are not in a healthy state. Overall, we are in decline.
b. On the other hand there are many very good and interesting things going on in the diocese at all levels.
c. Nevertheless, the overall state predominates over the many good things.
d. The many good things indicate that a different overall state may be possible. I believe some such an alternative would be closer to what God wants for this church.
e. Change is indicated.
f. Those outside, appear to have a variety of images of the Anglican church. On the positive side, my impression is that people welcome the churches getting into social justice issues,

> social welfare issues, and performing a chaplaincy role at times of national grief. But there is wariness about churches having too much influence in the political system, as indicated by the reactions to the former governor-general.[1] The sexual scandals and especially the churches' response to these scandals have damaged the standing of the churches in our society. As one of the churches, the Anglican Church attracts these positive and negative perceptions.
>
> Those outside see the Anglican Church made up of a rapidly aging group of people who find in the church support or encouragement to live some version of the good life, though, apart from 'church going', this 'good life' probably looks pretty much the way other people live.

This state of the Anglican Church in Melbourne, pictured in this image is a consequence of it having lost touch with a large part of the last three generations. Not just in the sense of numbers and age profile of those not involved in the church, but with their life-styles and cultures, with their different ways of being and relating as persons, with different spiritualities, sexualities and worldviews. These are the people whose lives are powerfully formed by the 'revolutions' that have marked our lives in the last forty years (see below), as distinct from earlier generations whose lives were formed in a different social context. In relation to these diverse currents of change, the overall life of the church is out of touch, notwithstanding the many changes that have also gone on in our church. For many of these people, the Anglican church is irrelevant.

Given this image, I seek something better for the Anglican Church, in Melbourne. This image suggests three tools that could help us to discern the something better. Firstly, in this image the Anglican church is not healthy. To go further we need some useful theological account of what is a healthy church. Secondly, part of the sickness of the church is due to its relationship with our society. We need some account of our society and the relationship of a healthy church to our society. Thirdly, the image claims that the overall life of this church

---

1. Another account of the churches having too much influence, is provided by D Marr, *The High Price of Heaven* (Melbourne: Allen & Unwin, 1999).

dominates over the many good things happening across the diocese. This directs attention to how the overall life of the church may be differently ordered. We need to think again about the ministry of oversight, of those bearing responsibility for the overall life of the church. For Anglicans this is the ministry of bishops. In this paper the first two matters will be considered while the third, which I have addressed elsewhere, will receive only fleeting reference.[2]

What makes for a healthy church? I take 'health' to mean wellbeing, indeed abundant wellbeing and I believe that scripture, theology, reason and commonsense would agree. In the light of scripture and theology what is the abundant wellbeing that ought to characterise a healthy church?

I believe that the wellbeing of the church is enhanced or diminished depending on whether and to what extent our way of being church aligns with, or goes against the grain of our being in Christ. Therefore I believe that the church's well being is in being faithful and fruitful: being faithful to the being and doing of God in Christ; being fruitful is what grows in, is produced by and results from being faithful. What shall we say of our being in Christ?

To guide an answer I draw on the Creed, where we say we believe in 'one, holy, catholic and apostolic church'.[3] I will use these four 'marks', though not in that order, to speak about the wellbeing that ought to characterise a healthy church and the *dissonances* and *resonances* we might expect to find between church and society.

Before doing so, however, I will present a view of our social context, which informs and is informed by the theological perspective intimated by speaking of a 'healthy' church. Not too much hangs on the order of presentation. The important point for me is that for theological reasons I want to imagine the wellbeing of the church only in the closest connection with imagining the well being of the world in

---

2. S Ames, 'Real Oversight or the Chimere of Episcope', in, A Cadwallader editor with D Richardson, *Episcopacy, Views from the Antipodes* (Melbourne: Anglican Board of Christian Education, 1994), 23–43; 'Assistant Bishops in the Diocese of Melbourne: The Tension between Centralism and Regionalism', in *The Culture of Melbourne Anglicanism and Anglicanism in Melbourne's Culture*, edited by C Holden (Melbourne: The History Department, The University of Melbourne, 2000).

3. I was happy to discover the precedent for this approach set by Hans Küng's, *The Church* (New York: Image Books, Doubleday, 1967), part D and sorry that I had not found it earlier.

which we live. Also, given the above picture of the Anglican church as I find it, there is good sense in first considering our social context. I conclude with some considerations about how we may live faithfully and fruitfully in the tensions entailed in the *dissonances* and *resonances* between church and society, when the church is becoming a healthy church.

2. Attending to the social context

These reflections on the social context are intended to be indicative and suggestive, rather than comprehensive. I will use three different levels of reflection. One is the *overt* 'in your face' level of turbulent change in the period following Second World War. This level of reflections refers to the multiplicity of phenomena and fashions of social change that criss-cross and churn up everyday life. In this paper I highlight a variety of 'revolutions' that have marked this period. The second level of reflection refers to more covert changes in and under the phenomena and the fashions of turbulent daily experience. These changes, initially covert and *insinuated*, start to become clearer in the wake of the turbulence. Thirdly there is a level of reflection referring to the *grounding assumptions* or grounding 'logic' of this turbulent social change.

2.1 Overt 'in your face' change

One way of conjuring up the 'in your face' experience of change is by talking about the 'revolutions' that have occurred in the period since the Second World War. Here are some examples; doubtless there are more:

- The continuing threat of weapons of mass destruction developed and stock-piled by many nations. The threat was vividly awakened by the bombs dropped by the US on Hiroshima and Nagasaki, on 6 and 9 August 1945. The threat is an issue in regard to the stability of Pakistan, the relation between Pakistan and India, the weapons possessed by Israel. The threat is most frequently raised in the relationship between the US and North Korea, though not with regard to Iraq despite claims to justify the war on Iraq
- Sexual revolution, starting with the pill in early 1960s; gay and lesbian movements

- Green revolution—strengthened after 1969 with the photo of the earth from the moon, but facing continuing ecological degradation; ozone hole on the road to recovery; greenhouse gas effects
- Feminist revolution: 19th century women's movements; feminism from the 1970s, followed by successive waves
- Technological revolution—a product of twentieth century new science; post the Second World War; computers; NASA
- Communication revolution, especially TV; satellites; optical fibre; mobile phone; internet
- 'Free' market revolution; extension of market relations to more and more of life; signalled in the development of global financial markets and rapid, deregulated movement of vast amounts of capital; the replacement of skilled and unskilled manual labour with higher productivity of new technology; accelerates the commodification of more and more of life; relatedly, the collapse of state communism in Russia
- Genetic engineering revolution; human genome project; biotechnology; cloning; stem cell research
- Nano revolution, machines on a micro, micro scale taking over and remaking our lives.

In addition, we should think of the arms trade and drug trade, as well as the abuse of children, the impact of unpayable debt, the scourges of poverty, hunger and AIDS, and the increasing gap between wealthy and poor nations. Some of these changes have provided the focus for a number of social movements, most recently the movements against the globalisation as we know it.

In this period since the Second World War we should especially refer to the growing voices of Aboriginal and other Australians seeking to acknowledge our history and work for reconciliation, even though that movement has stalled under the present federal government; the change from White Australia to a multicultural Australia to the recent response of the government (with no real alternative from the Labour opposition) to refugees and asylum seekers and the 'wedge' politics that goes with it; the change from a widely valued egalitarian society, with strong public sector in a mixed economy, to a society encompassed by the 'free market' with a growing division between the very affluent and powerful strata, and those who are being left behind with regard to employment, education, health–care and housing; the division between urban and rural Australia; the many changes in the place of women in Australian society and so in the relations between women and men.

The most 'in your face' experience of change, for people in the West, was the September 11 attack on the US and the resulting war on terrorism. The '9/11' attack was focused on destroying the symbolic order of the US (Trade Towers, Pentagon, White House(?)), a symbolic order representing the global economic, military, political and cultural dominance of the US, a dominance profoundly hated and mocked by the attackers. The resulting war on terrorism lead to at least three related, 'in your face' experience of change in Australia and other nations.

One is the state's increased power of surveillance of people, the increased threat of terrorist attack with the still greater, politically induced fear of this threat and the sense of insecurity about the way life is going.

Another is the heightened politics of division, following Mr Bush's challenge to all nations, 'you are either with us or with the terrorists', found a rich field of opportunities in the United Nations. Australia was divided about our support of the US in the war on Afghanistan and then on Iraq. We were at war without war being declared and again young Australians were sent off to fight in the name of a divided Australia. In a massive turn out Australians joined people around the world in protesting against this war. There are parallels and differences between the response to this military involvement and the turbulent division in Australia about our government's support for the US in Vietnam. Both stand in contrast to the strong public support for our military role in the UN mission to secure an independent East Timor.[4]

The third is what has happened to Australia and its politics. The war on Iraq was pursued under the doctrine of preemptive strike, and not withstanding international law, was allegedly justified by Iraq's possession of and capacity rapidly to deploy weapons of mass destruction as well as pass them to Al-queda. This was questioned in the lead

4. This support reflects the longstanding public dissatisfaction within Australia about our government's stance towards the Suharto government and the Indonesian military. This was fuelled by our lack of support for East Timor under Indonesian rule.

up to the war. Subsequent investigations have not turned up any WMD. The government has now invoked the deposing of Saddam Hussein as the humanitarian justification of the war. This is amazing given the history of US support for Hussein including allowing him to stay if he had disarmed Iraq; the UN sanctions that contained Iraq while killing Iraqis and provided scope for Saddam to terrorise and kill them; the fact that dictatorships from Burma to Saudi Arabia are allowed to continue because no foreign policy 'analogy' obtains; and our indefinitely detaining Iraqis and Afghanis fleeing these regimes because they have jumped a 'queue' (though no analogy obtains) and are maybe terrorists. We continue to be misled about the reasons for war by our government that speaks as if it occupied the 'high ground', both morally and intellectually. That speaking is largely justified by pointing to the horrors of terrorism and Saddam Hussein's rule in Iraq. The trouble is if you pick a standard lower enough anything looks good.

These comments help mark out the contemporary conditions under which we live life on planet earth. But there are at least two other levels of change going on.

2.2 Covert, insinuated change

If we stay at this overt level of change we will have plenty to think about and do, but we need to move onto consider other things that may help us live more faithfully and fruitfully under contemporary conditions. To borrow from St Paul, we may see in the daily phenomena of turbulent change 'another law at work', maybe several. This is what I want to highlight now and at other points in this paper.

At the overt level one can often find, in the media and in many conversations, the view that the only thing we can be certain about is that change is always with us, and everyone will have to adapt and adjust. This seems so true that **turbulent change has come to be treated as 'natural',** as if such change was a force of nature. This attitude to change is so obvious that it is not even noticed. It is simply insinuated. It leads to forgetting the past, to focusing on the latest emerging new wave of the future. This is fed by technological, commodity and consumption imperatives and so reverse Kant's dictum: *can implies must, so just do it!* This change process is a virulent natualism.

This understanding may be elaborated using the work of Australian scientist and philosopher, Cliff Hooker.[5] Hooker argues that in a stable environment, organisms whose biological resources go to producing more offspring, which leads to greater adaptation, do best overall. In a changing environment, organisms whose biological resources go to make for greater adaptability, which means greater complexity, do best overall. Hooker thinks that these insights into biological evolution hold true for social and cultural change. He also thinks that since the scientific revolution, a 'huge societal change engine' has come into being characterised by a dominant form of inquiry, which proceeds by probing and disturbing the physical environment and seeing what happens. The probing includes the technological extension of human capacities. This mode of learning eventually leads to an increasingly changing social and ecological environment. In response to this accelerating change, those people who happen to be equipped with greater adaptability to such change will fare better overall than those who have pursued greater adaptation to their environment and enjoy different modes of knowing, which may include this 'probing' form of inquiry in limited ways, certainly not as dominant. These especially include people with their roots in pre-modern societies, including tribal societies.

Though I cannot here review the relevant historical development, I do want to add to Hooker's view the qualification that the 'huge societal change engine' has come into existence as commodity production and market exchange develop and interact with this form of inquiry. Production and market exchange are powerfully informed by the continuing development of technologies, which this form of empirical inquiry makes possible. Eventually this interaction leads towards convergence: inquiry is increasingly directed by the interests of the dominance of commodity exchange and the production that serves it and is served by it.

On Hooker's model it is people with greater capacity for adaptability and who continue to invest their resources in developing this capacity who survive and thrive best in such a changing social context. But this context is then further biased in their favour by their initiating

---

5. Cliff Hooker, at the University of New Castle. See his 'Between Formalism and Anarchy: A Reasonable Middle Way', in *Beyond Reason*, G Munevar, editor (Dordretch: Kluwer, 1991).

or contributing to new changes that pursue this mode of 'probing' inquiry, and so further destabilise the social and ecological environment. Clearly there will also be those not favoured by this process.

The 'societal change engine' is now drawing individuals, organisations and nations into a vast global change process that both maintains these distinctions and rewrites them. On this model we can envisage how these different kinds of participants show a similar range of responses to this turbulent change, forming a spectrum from highly advantaged to highly disadvantaged. Here I group different kinds of responses by individuals in Australia.

First, people who have the adaptability to embrace this turbulent social environment and thrive within it. One thinks of highly mobile, young, cosmopolitan 'knowledge workers'. They are adepts in using the state of the art of this mode of inquiry in various fields, the knowledge and technology it produces, and who have access to increasing wealth and other resources needed to employ and develop this 'state of the art'. Adaptability is not just for one generation. People from the preceding generations with established wealth, education and inclination, are also able to thrive within this turbulent social environment.

Second, people who reject this form of life. For example: successful participants in the 'knowledge economy' down-shifting out of the ratrace; people from the preceding generations who consciously pursue an alternative to both this form of life and that of an earlier era; young people also exploring alternative life-styles, including those whose body piercing, clothing, and 'tribal' forms of association symbolise their alternative. They all variously survive and thrive, with the latter thriving more precariously. An important instance in Australia of this kind of response is a number of Indigenous communities which have made a significant reappropriation of their heritage as part of an increased individual and communal adaptability in the present environment of change.

Thir, older people who remember a different form of life, marked by a greater degree of face-to-face contact, and a greater reliance on tradition and institutions. These people go some way to retaining that form of life within their circle of friends and family, in work and leisure and community associations. They make some use of the benefits of new technologies. For some people this adaptation is lived with a strong sense of nostalgia and may merge with the following grouping.

Fourth, the people who survive, but do not thrive. These are the many people underemployed or unemployed and the people who are over-employed in the sense of overworked. Despite material prosperity, at least for those employed, even many of them are unhappy or at least ambivalent about the way they have to live under contemporary conditions.

Fifth, the people whose survival is at risk or lost, who have limited resources, who cannot see any opportunity for themselves amidst the turbulent social change. For example, people in various kinds of addiction, whether alcohol, other drugs, or problem gambling, as well as the many youth suicides and the larger number of attempted suicides. Here we must include Indigenous people whose communities suffered horribly from their first encounters with those whose acquired identity, worldview and skills, gave them a competitive advantage, in the destabilised environment of *their* making and who have not been able to re-appropriate their traditions.

Those who are most advantaged will instantiate an uneven leading edge of social change processes. Those occupying this position will increasingly control, concentrate and consume more resources to ensure the elaboration of a still greater adaptability (and therewith a greater self-preoccupation) and to maintain and escalate the rate and directions of change. In this lies their advantage. This ensures that those with less adaptability, less able to 'move on' will be further disadvantaged. This dominance will be maintained by protecting access, including the use of force, to the human and material resources needed to retain the advantage. Those in this leading edge position will also ensure the dominance of their life-styles and understanding of life via the media that serves the convergence of inquiry, commodity production and market exchange noted above. For those in that position, the prospects engendered by this process have 'no limits'. People and organisations with global reach and power, who enjoy this advantage, are elaborating a 'world order' within and across nations, in order to maintain the advantage. This is a systemic consequence, of the 'change engine' not a conspiracy.

Analogous consequences are also discernable within and between nations, where there is an increasing gap between those advantaged and those disadvantaged by this change process. From the position of those advantaged, many of the disadvantaged will become dispensable, eventually becoming invisible, unrecognized, as they are left behind and lost in the waste products of the turbulent change process. Australian history offers the fictional term 'terra nullius' as a metaphor for this repeated effect of the change process.

Among those who reject this form of life are those who hate its dominance, especially its dominant culture and symbolic order, and including making dispensable the disadvantaged. Among those who hate its dominance some pursue violent opposition in acts of terror. Among those most disadvantaged by the change process, some resist the way their life is going by attempting to cross national borders as refugees in order to access even the crumbs of the 'good life' of the advantaged.

2.3 Grounding assumptions

Here I can only indicate rather than argue for these views. The immediate starting point for this reflection on our social context is that this turbulent social change is now treated as 'natural', as if it were a force of nature. In Hooker's view this is a correct description, since it is the continuation of the *same* processes as are seen in evolutionary biology.

I think the grounding assumption of this change process is one expression of naturalism. In much contemporary philosophy, naturalism is the view that what the natural sciences says there is, is all there is, and that methods used in scientific inquiry are the best or even the only ways of finding out about the world and ourselves as part of the world. This objectifying approach to the world aims to give a completely naturalistic account of human life. In this view the world has no intrinsic point and therefore no intrinsic value. Rather, both epistemic and moral values, which guide our inquiries and our relating to each other, are understood instrumentally.[6]

My view is that our culture inscribes in us the naturalistic view of the world as the taken-for-granted habit of thought about the kind of

---

6. As the physicist and Nobel Laureate S Weinberg famously remarked, 'the more the universe seems comprehensible the more it also seems pointless'. S Weinberg, *The First Three Minutes* (New York: Basic Books, 1977), 155. Likewise, as Dawkins says, the evolutinary process is blind, see R Dawkins, *The Blind Watchmaker* (London: Penguin, 1986). But note there is no simple connection between this worldview and the ethics that may be espoused. For example, R Dawkins does not live by the selfish gene, has no account of his own ethics, thinks humankind is alone able to rise above the gene regime. A point made by Dr Keith Ward in a recent visit to Australia.

world this is in which we live. Consequently the absence of intrinsic point and value becomes the 'truth' about human life. Yet human beings seek a sense of the meaning and value of their lives as if intrinsic. This contradiction opens the way for something else to be the exquisite surrogate of intrinsic point and value of life. This ensures that any surrogate fulfils and frustrates the seeking. For example, when the surrogate is commodity consumption people become 'consumers' who can never have enough. This state is now achieved by the time children reach pre-school. On the other hand the felt absence of intrinsic value and point can lead to various kinds of spiritual awakenings that in turn may lead to the critical dropping out noted above, or may help people simply 'keep going', or may turn into a spiritual market place, coopted into the paths of commodity consumption. A third example is the dominance of instrumental value shown in what I call the 'two great commandments' of the change process: you only have value if you add value; you only get value if you pay for it.

2.4 Summary

The daily phenomena of turbulent change are generated by a 'societal change engine' that arose 400 hundred years ago in Europe and is formed by the convergence of a particular mode of inquiry, the technologies thereby made available, commodity production and market exchange. This 'change engine' continuously destabilizes the environment, favouring those equipped with the capacity to enhance their adaptability to change, over those equipped for adaptation to a given environment. This has led to a globalised social Darwinism, a virulent life form delivering unprecedented material affluence for those able to adapt and leaving in its wake the debris of those who cannot. This form of life is expansionary an now is pervasive. Its 'logic' is in effect what according to political theory is called 'sovereign power'—that power of which there is none greater. One expression of this power is the widely taken-for-granted assumption that all this is 'natural'. The grounding assumptions on which it operates are well represented philosophically by naturalism, including the view that the world has no intrinsic point or value.

First interlude

It would of course be possible to go straight to discussing *resonances* and *dissonances* between church and society. For example, the above discussion of *grounding assumptions* surely points to a *dissonance* between church and society. Possibly. But what if a church is 'positioned' such that it too is now operating from a large dose of naturalism, and what if its spirituality has been co-opted as a form of consumption, or what if the church is enculturated in such a way that it suffers from amnesia and is a caricature of the gospel? Some people in the church have a 'commodity' approach to the gospel. They think we have a terrific product, which we are not selling properly. A different instance would be the 'positioning' of the churches in supporting the colonial and later federal and state governments' treatment of Indigenous communities.

The problem in going straight to a discussion of *resonances* and *dissonances* is that it too much takes for granted the position from which to pursue that response. It assumes we are already 'positioned' by the gospel, that we are able to reflect and act in its light. If this assumption is incorrect, then any church that holds it is at best naïve and at risk of being caught in *resonances* and *dissonances* with the society in which it lives, but not on account of the gospel.

In this paper I count it necessary to take time to elaborate a position from which to make a more thoughtful and active response to the social context envisaged above.[7]

3. A theological vignette on a healthy church

Recalling the introduction, I believe that the wellbeing of the church is enhanced or diminished depending on whether and to what extent our

---

7. This point also concerns the forms of theological reflection. I believe there are at least five forms of reflection. a) Interpreting experience in the light of one's faith. b) Handling the contradictions between one's experience and one's faith. c) Elaborating one's theological resources. d) Critically integrating one's theological and non-theological resources for reflection. e) Most importantly, establishing what is normative for one's theology. We need to work on all five forms of reflection. Each of each of these forms of reflection is indicated in what follows. A further important issue is what the theological reflection actually reflects. Does it reflect by rationalising a situation or does it reflect the God who will allow no one to boast, as in Jeremiah 9:23–24?

way of being church aligns with, or goes against the grain of our being in Christ. What shall we say of our being in Christ?

To guide an answer I draw on the Creed where we say we believe in 'one, holy, catholic and apostolic church.' I will use these four 'marks', though not in that order, to speak about the wellbeing that ought to characterise a healthy church and the *dissonances* and *resonances* we might expect to find between church and society.

3.1 We believe in one, holy, catholic and apostolic church[8]

The church is one

'Joined to Christ by the power of the Spirit, Christians enjoy fellowship both with God the Father and with one another.' Through this grace of God, *'the church is constituted by the participation of its members in the communion of the life of the triune God.'*[9]

Unity in the Spirit

We share in the divine life by the power of the Spirit, for it is by the Spirit that our hearts are opened to hear the good news of Christ calling us to new life; that we are led to acknowledge Jesus as Lord and Saviour, that we are baptised into Christ; that we give thanks for the death and resurrection of our Lord, and together eat and drink his body and blood; that we read, mark, learn and inwardly digest the scriptures to shape our faith and our lives; that we maintain the common faith and fellowship of the church; that we fully enter into the mission of God in and for the world.

Unity in diversity

The unity of the church is a unity in diversity, a dynamic unity which gives 'individuals, and local communities, and different traditions, scope to be fully themselves'[10] as together they pursue the mission of God.

---

8. From the Nicene Creed. I will highlight what I think are a few crucial aspects of each mark. For the purpose of this paper I treat the second mark last.
9. *Episcopal Ministry: The Report of the Archbishop's Group on the Episcopate* (London: Church House, 1990), 158.
10. *Ibid*, 8.

Only so does the church build itself up to the stature of the fullness of Christ and only so can it have access to and be a foretaste of the dynamic unity and diversity of the life of God. The diversity of the gifts of the Spirit which are distributed to all the members of the church are to be fully expressed because they are essential to the constitution of the church as the body of Christ and thus to fulfilling its part in the mission of God in and for the world.

Community of communities in Christ

The church is a communion of communities in which the whole, who is Christ, is in each of the parts.[11] On this basis each community, being in communion with all the other communities of the church, has access to the fullness of God, who in Christ, dwells in each community and each community in God. Again, when all the communities of the body of Christ are working together, the body is built up until it attains the full stature of Christ.

The church is a communion of communities in which the whole, who is Christ, is in each of the parts. Our being in Christ is therefore a holographic unity, marked by a distinctive eccentricity, synergy and creativity, by subsidiarity and a sense of what counts as a 'local' church when the church is also universal.

Eccentricity

For this reason the unity of the church is marvellously eccentric, in that the only 'centre', who is the triune God, is accessible to the smallest as to the largest Christian communities, as each and all maintain the unity of the church. For the same reason the unity of the church is not

---

11. See John 15:5, 'I am the vine, you are the branches'. Christ is the 'whole', we are the 'parts', though here the whole is not only more than the sum of the parts, the whole precedes the parts and is not obtained by bringing the parts together. Also the theological motif of the 'body of *Christ*' is so different from 'body' used metaphorically of a group of people. Again, this motif highlights Christ, not just as 'head' but as the whole whose members (parts) we are. We can see this also from the diverse applications of '*ekklesia*' (church) in 1 Corinthians 1:2, 11:22, 12:28; Romans 16:16; Acts 20. 'The term has been transformed [from classical and contemporary Greek usage and even from its distinctive meaning in the Hebrew Bible] . . . to describe a body of men and women in which the unity of every part corresponds to, repeats, represents and is the unity of the whole.' (E Hoskins and N Davey, *The Riddle of the New Testament* (London: Faber and Faber, 1958).

'arithmetic', the sum of its parts, nor 'radial' like the spokes of a wheel to some would-be 'centre',[12] nor 'bureaucratic', as if the church were merely an organisation to be rationally administered.

Synergy and creativity

Râther, the church is a community of communities, and the communities that make up the church are to live out a deepening interdependence that is essential to their proper self-understanding and to their wellbeing. This is because, though often poorly realised and sometimes betrayed in practice, we have been admitted to a new order in Christ in which we are interdependent. This new order in Christ is grounded in and open to the reciprocity and mutuality of the triune God. This draws us into ever-new *synergies* of communion and cooperation, which evokes an abundant creativity, which has its 'measure': 'thirty-fold, sixty-fold, a hundred-fold'. This is the strength and vitality we are given for mission.

The church as institution is to serve the church as community

'To stress that the church is communal is to emphasise relationships; the personal is thus prior to the institutional; the institutional exists to nurture and sustain relationships of human persons joined, as far as possible for us creatures, in a resemblance to [the] Trinitarian life.'[13]

The personal, meaning persons in community, has priority over the institutional; the institutional is to serve the personal.[14] Elsewhere scripture says we now see as through a 'glass darkly', but then we will see 'face to face'. Even the embodied, face-to-face character of the Christian community is to be a sign of the glory that is coming, already at work in us.

The more obvious implications of this have to do with the way we handle our politics, the way the institution makes decisions about individuals, the way we handle conflicts between individuals and groups, the ways we can be more accountable to one another that are

---

12. Not that these could not be a 'centre' just that it would have to represent the centricity of the living God, who is marvellously eccentric.

13. *Episcopal Ministry* (1990), 8.

14. In this respect what was said of the sabbath applies to other institutions; see Mark 2:2728.

constructive, even life-giving, the quality of our speaking to and about one another, especially when the 'other' is absent.

Summary

These and other themes to do with our unity in Christ need further theological reflection. But we can see that:

- The wellbeing of the church depends on whether our way of being church is aligned with our being in Christ.
- The vitality and creativity of our life and our living authority for mission as a church and as churches depend on our enjoying rather than blocking our shared access to the fullness of Christ, who therefore do not quench the Spirit.
- This is so both ecumenically and within the Anglican church, for there is only one church.
- Shared access to the fullness of Christ is a gift that comes to the church from the Spirit through the interdependence of all the parts working together, both as communities and people within communities.
- Where the church is weak it is because we see in our members another law at work from the one we say we approve.

The church is catholic

> *'All authority in heaven and on earth has been given to me, go therefore and make disciples of all nations, baptizing them in the name of the Father and of the Son and of the Holy Spirit.'*[15]

The church has received this great commission and it is one key measure of the catholicity of the church. If the church lacks the breadth measured by the great commission it is too narrow, too partial, and in its members there will again be found another law at work, besides this 'law' of Christ.

The great commission sets no limit on who is to be met with the gospel and baptised. The same is true of 'the many' in the word over the eucharistic cup. If anyone thinks in terms of numbers, percentages, optimal size, the only scriptural answer is 'everyone!' If someone bids us be 'realistic', the answer is that the gospel is precisely about what

15. Matthew 28: 18–19.

counts as 'reality'. If someone says we cannot 'go it alone', the answer is that we never thought of going it alone.

Rather, this task is accomplished in the Spirit, by Christian communities around the world that are the bearers and interpreters of the gospel. They provide the means whereby people come to faith and grow in faith, as reconciled to God and members one of another in Christ. The catholicity of the church is especially to be seen in ecumenical cooperation in response to the great commission.

Therefore, given the diversity of people's cultures, subcultures, lifestyles and generational differences, the church needs to radically multiply the number and diversify the forms of Christian community in order that it may fulfill the great commission. Something of this diversity of communities could be elaborated in terms of size, location, both geographic and non-geographic, leadership, ethos and replication. The diversity means there will be very large mega-churches, solid traditional parishes, both large and small, and a myriad of other 'travelling light' communities.

Recognising the reality of *resonances* and *disonnaces* between the gospel and the society in which the church lives, the making and sustaining of people as disciples of Christ, is especially important.

The church is apostolic

'As the Father has sent me so I send you.' When he had said this he breathed on them and said, 'Receive the Holy Spirit . . .'[16]

The whole church is sent out into the world where God is already at work, albeit often incognito. The whole church is to make known the good news of Christ and to embody his life in every aspect of the life of the world. The whole church is to do this in continuity with the church of the apostles, and therefore in handing on, in a living way, their teaching, fellowship, the breaking of bread and prayers.

Going on beyond the present

Firstly, within the continuity just noted, the apostolicity of the church is also demonstrated in our going beyond where we have reached to date, into every aspect of life, to all people, where we have been sent.[17]

---

16. John 20:
17. In the spirit of 2 Corinthians 10:12–18.

This should be a continuing, visible mark of our life as an apostolic church. One possible concrete expression of this should be evident in what is intuited and envisaged, as well as in what is planned and implemented, both in the short term and the long term, at all levels and in every part of the church, and frequently issuing in bold initiatives. And it would surely be evident in a felt sense of shared momentum as we move on together, being led by the Spirit.

There are some indications of this orientation, but overall it is still far from being a consistent and enabling part of our apostolate and consequently we live with a sense of fitful momentum at best. The overall state of the church still dominates. Thankfully, some bold initiatives do arise in the life of the church. I pray that they flourish even more! Imagine living with an encompassing sense of 'momentum' that carried us all forward!

Discipleship and apostleship

Secondly, the church is called to follow Christ on the way and to learn from him. The disciples 'learned Christ' by a robust conversation with Jesus and amongst themselves, concerning the coming of the reign of God, who he is, his teaching, his mighty works, his authority, the meaning of the scriptures and the traditions which they inherited, how they are to pray, their relationships with him and each other, and about what they experienced on the way. Now this earlier 'conversation' is to be remembered and repeated anew in the Spirit of Jesus, both within and between the churches, concerning these very same things. The church is called to be a community of disciples who continue to learn and to learn from one another.

Given what has been said so far about the marks of a healthy church, there is a great need to go on learning together, both within and between all the 'parts' that make up the church. To borrow an apt phrase from the world, the church could be a stunning example of a learning organisation,[18] better, a learning community. Surely the community of disciples is to be a discipleship community?

---

18. P Senge, *The Fifth Discipline* (London: Doubleday Currency, 1995). As an example of learning together, what can we learn from the use across the diocese of Alpha, Catechumenate, Credo, and other ways of introducing people to faith in Christ and membership of the church?

Learning and unlearning

There is also some unlearning to do. Earlier it was said that the wellbeing of the church is in being faithful and fruitful. Of course, being fruitful depends on being faithful. But is it possible to be faithful and not fruitful? If it turns out that some person or community believes it is faithful but not fruitful, the presumption, based on scripture, is that there is a story yet to be told, as to why they are not being fruitful or why the fruit is not being recognised.[19]

What we must not do is to rationalise being unfruitful as normal, nor spiritualise it as our faithfully carrying the 'cross of Christ', nor yet resign ourselves to it, with all the scope for isolation, bad conscience, desperation and cynicism that such resignation carries, as if being faithful could still survive under these conditions. This highlights one important kind of unlearning that may be needed. Rather, we must tell the story that waits to be told and so learn what is needed for being fruitful as well as faithful.

Second interlude

The first mark spoke about our being in Christ on the assumption that our way of being church can go with or against the grain of our being in Christ. This determines the degree to which the church has access to the fullness of Christ and therewith all that is needed to fulfil its mission and its engagement with the world. The next two marks spoke of this engagement with the world through the church being sent into all the world with the same mission as Christ, with one result being more and more people from all the nations believing and being baptised. The next mark to be considered speaks about the relationship of the church and the world modelled on the relation between Christ and the world as one of *dissonance* and *resonance*. This takes us further into the engagement of the church and the world on account of sharing in the same mission as Christ.

---

19. Eg see Mark 4:1520.

The church is holy

'In response to Jesus, the demons cried out "What have you to do with us Jesus of Nazareth? Have you come to destroy us? I know who you are, the Holy One of God!"'[20]

From scripture and tradition, I should say that being faithful and fruitful is what ought to characterise humankind created to enjoy the original blessing of being made in the image of God, to hear God speaking in many ways, calling us all to seek our life with God, to live justly and graciously with each other, enjoying the 'original blessing' in exercising an awesome dominion over the earth—though not over each other—as stewards who are the image and likeness of the living God who created the world.[21] Furthermore, the whole created order is good, yet still incomplete, being destined by God for a still greater goodness.

In fact it is another orientation, with other possibilities of life, to which we listen most carefully and are led by more persuasively, while maybe ensuring there is a 'place' for God or the gods, unless we have come to see ourselves in a godless world. In any of its forms, this other orientation of individual and social life eventually comes to be established as having a life of its own, an encompassing 'fiction'[22] more living us than being lived by us; a surrogate of true life, with its

---

20. Mark 1: 23–24.
21. It is the distortion of this 'dominion' after the counter-image of the living God that is the source of the run-away human ecology and economy with its destruction of species, pollution and global warming. The answer is to direct not deny human powers.
22. In discussion some people find this use of the term 'fiction' unsatisfactory. It fails to convey the reality to which it points. Patriachy would surely count as 'fictions', but for some it is a distortion that is real and a lie and so a 'fiction'. I will continue to use the term, which for me has all the power of a lived reality that is a distortion and to the extent that it is but not more, it is also a lie. For a similar use of the term 'fiction', see Frank Brennan's book, *Sharing the Country* (London: Penguin, 1991), 19. 'This legal fiction of *terra nullius* became firmly embedded in our history. Though a fiction, it has taken on a reality of its own that cannot be undone.' For a recent theological discussion of living a 'lie', see A. Shanks discussion of V Havel's parable of the grocer shop in Havel's essay, 'The Power of the Powerless' (English translation by P Wilson), in *Living in Truth,* edited by J Vladislav (London: Faber & Faber, 1987), 41. See A Shanks, *God and Modernity, a New and Better Way to Do Theology* (London: Routledge, 2000), 1.

own economy, ecology and even theology, that possesses, shapes, flavours and directs our living, as if it had a life of its own. In any of its forms, this other orientation of individual and social life establishes a field of *dissonances* and *resonances* between the 'fiction' by which it lives and the life to which everyone is called by God.

This surrogate of true life in effect comes to assume the role of divinity: it defines the taken-for-granted 'reality'; it becomes that in which we practically live and move and have our being; it forms people from birth, or in the context of invaders and occupiers who are the carriers of their own 'divinity', it takes over and makes-over people, reforming them, in its own image; it rewards those that fit in, but demeans those it does not recognise, those that oppose it or do not fit, those for whom there is no room.[23] Producing and becoming a 'creature' of this surrogate 'divinity' continues to be humankind's own most original sin.

Yet for all this life, remains a great and precious gift that God, *incognito*, is everywhere at work to bring to its senses. There are many that still sense how precious is the gift of life, whether and however they conceive of the Giver. They too are a sign of God secretly working 'against the grain' to awaken people everywhere to the gift of life and to the love that has created them and calls them on.[24]

Something of this may be seen in the life of Israel, God's people from of old. At God's calling, the prophets of Israel denounced the violent mis-ordering of the nation's life, the worship of idols, the 'chewing up'[25] of the poor by the powerful, the want of the knowledge of God, shown in the want of justice, and the warning of exile. Later there are warnings of the 'beastly' dominion of foreign occupation of the land and the enforced worship of foreign gods. The same prophets looked for a time when the most humane reign of the living God would come, and the 'beastly' rule would be overcome.[26] Yet because

---

23. For more on a 20c globalised version of such 'divinity', see Harvey Cox, 'Living in the New Dispensation', *Ministry Society and Theology*, Vol 14, No. 2, 2000.
24. A question for some will be whether I intend to include Indigenous communities in these terms as well. The answer is that I do, though with very different *dissonances* and *resonances* between their form of life and the life to which God call us all, and those that are displayed in twenty-first century Western societies.
25. Micah 3:1–3.
26. Daniel 7.

of this disorder, the whole creation is disordered with respect to the divine purpose in creation.

The apostles, evangelists and seers of the church tell of this promise being realised in Jesus the Messiah, in whom the most humane reign of the living God comes into the world. This good news tells of the promised redemption and the fulfillment of the created order by that still greater goodness intended from the beginning, but only lately seen in its astonishing beauty and fullness in Christ.[27] At great cost this one and only future has been opened for all, now in anticipation, yet finally in glory. This has taken place through the mission of Jesus, the incarnate Word. Sent by the Father in the power of the Spirit, Jesus makes present the reign of God and so enters into vulnerable but victorious conflict with the powers of life misoriented and established falsely as a life of its own. It turns out that he triumphs[28] over these powers that bar entry to the reign of God. The relationship of Jesus the Messiah to the world is one of *dissonance* and *resonance.*

Dissonance and resonance: Christ and the world

There is a profound *dissonance* or mismatch between what Jesus shows to be the truth about the world and what the world takes to be the truth about itself. This is the *dissonance* between, on the one hand, the realities of the reign of God proclaimed and made present through Jesus, the definitive, though not exclusive, foretaste of the only future that comes from God. On the other, those encompassing, worldly 'fictions', the taken-for-granted 'realities' in which we come to live and move and have our being. This *dissonance* is most acute in the crucifixion and resurrection of Jesus, including all the conflict, betrayal and desertion, leading to his execution, the price paid for being and opening the way into the only future intended for all things from the beginning.

There is a profound *resonance* or match between the realities of the reign of God, proclaimed and made present through Jesus, and the realities of the world created from the excess of divine love exchanged between the persons of the triune God. In its created being, the world

27. Matthew 25:34; Ephesians 1:10, 3:9–11.

28. Colossians 2:15. Here is divine authority. In this triumph, Jesus the Messiah is God's 'Yes' to all his promises for humanity and humanity's 'Amen' to God. (2 Cor.1:18–20) This fine theological motif is taken from *The Gift of Authority,* the third statetement on authority by the Anglican-Roman Catholic International Commission (ARCIC III).

is very good and intended for a still greater goodness. This *resonance* is shown in the true humanity of the Word incarnate, in Jesus being faithful and fruitful to the end—in bearing the gospel and the power of the reign of God, in withstanding temptation, in applauding the lilies, in healing and in forgiving sin, in vivid table fellowship with the rich and the poor, the righteous and the sinners, in life and death, in bodily resurrection as the first-born from the dead, in human flesh radiating divine glory. Yet more is involved. This place of acute *dissonance* is surely also a profound *resonance* between the suffering of God in Christ and the suffering of humankind subject to the powers of the encompassing fictions.

But against this claimed *resonance*, allegedly so profound, there may be heard what seems to be a deeper mocking *dissonance* between these human sufferings and the idea of the world being created from the excess of divine love exchanged between the persons of the triune God. The irony may even express itself theologically, 'with God all things are possible!' For many, this *dissonance* has eaten away, dissolved and so made impossible any idea of this world being created with a purposeful love by a holy God.

But this 'impossibility' is possible. The good news of God in Christ eventually leads us to understand that the world is created from the excess of divine love, and for love's sake, must do so by making things make themselves. And while this 'making themselves' might take more than one form, in our world one form it has taken is the evolutionary process of natural selection, which has all the appearances of having so much waste, pain and suffering, and of being purposeless, futile.[29] The fact that this process, with elements of

---

29. This idea of 'creation makes itself' was used by Christian Darwinians in the late nineteenth century, including Charles Kingsley in his *The Water Babies* (London: Hodder & Stoughton 1930, original edition 1863), 248. "Tom to the mother of creation, 'I heard you were always making new beasts out of old.' 'So people fancy', she said, 'I make things make themselves.'." Cited by Charles Birch i, 'Neo-Darwinism, Self-Organisation and Divine Action in Evolution', in *Evolutionary and Molecular Biology, Scientific Perspectives on Divine Action,* edited by RJ Russell, WR Stoeger, SJ, and F Ayala (Vatican City: Observatory, Vatican Observatory and Center for Theology and the Natural Sciences, Berkeley, 1998), 225. Birch writes, 'Four years after Charles Darwin published *The Origin of Species* the Church of England vicar and novelist, Charles Kingsley wrote for his children the evolutionary fairy tale *The Water Babies.* Kingsley was

convinced that the Darwinian theory of evolution was the context within which it was possible to find the working of "a living, immanent, ever-working God". The concept of God immanent in creation was understood by Kingsley as a creation in which "God makes things make themselves".' (*Ibid*, 225). As far as I know Kingsley gave no independent theological justification for this view. It is important to consider whether some such justification is available. Aubrey Moore, a contemporary of Kingsley's and another high church Anglican, dispensed with secondary causes and attribute the whole of the evolutionary process to the immanent working of the Logos whose incarnation in Jesus, Christianity proclaimed God. This may have been an attractive weapon to use against deism and pantheism and one can well understand Moore saying that Darwinism 'in the guise of a foe did the work of a friend'. [C Gore, editor, *Lux Mundi*, (London: John Murray, 1904), 75.] But until Darwin came along, no theologians thought of God acting in the world in a way that the world would look to detailed observation, anything like what was proposed by Darwin's theory of natural selection and the enormous amount of data it could explain. Were More and Kingsley simply making an ad hoc 'theory-change'? I think not. More thought Darwinism gave evidence of the immanent working in the world of that *Logos* whose incarnation is proclaimed by the Christian gospel. But still, why would God choose to create life on planet earth in such a way? Not everyone thinks that theology is under an obligation to explain this change in the theological account of the way God works in the world. But by way of comparison, I think that the author of Luke-Acts goes to considerable lengths to explain theologically why it is that the gentile inheritors of the promises were turning out to be different from the original recipients. It is the God of Abraham, Isaac and Jacob, is the God who now has made Jesus Messiah and Lord. I think that there is a need for some relevant insight into God's way of creating such as is provided by St Thomas Aquinas [*Summa Theologiae*, 1a. 22. 3; 1a. 103.6; 1a. 105.5.] Because God is the very essence of goodness, says Aquinas, we should speak of God in terms of superlatives. Therefore we should say that God makes things with real causal powers; that God gives to things the dignity of also being causes, rather than the indignity of also not being causes; that it is better that things are not only good in themselves but also the cause of good in other things. On similar grounds we should say that God maximises these features of creation rather than minimises them. Therefore we should expect that things make other things and that overall creation makes itself. How God as a rational creator might choose to realise such a creation is something to be known by observation. In our world an abundance of observation shows this includes evolution by natural selection. Thus it is because God is all-powerful, all-knowing, wholly good, that creation takes place by means of evolution according to natural selection, with all the suffering and waste this involves. Theologically this exemplifies the best that God could do. These comments bear on the issue of theodicy, by seeking(!) some theological insight cooperation as well as competition, eventually produces a multitude of beautiful and extraordinary creatures, including humankind, does not contradict these appearances. The fact that humankind, with its extraordinary powers, produces much that is good, true and beautiful, does not prevent the overwhelming human history of power, violence, pain and suffering, from challenging, weakening and even under-mining many people's belief about the world being created by a purposeful love. Or so it appears.

But in the light of the good news, these appearances, for all their power and finality concerning God are neither the first nor the last word. For this love's sake the processes of 'making things make themselves' must run its course. This 'making things make themselves' includes the evolutionary process bringing forth humankind as the new reality of *persons* who can only really exist as persons in relation. And then the history of 'making things make themselves' must follow a long and ongoing bloody history of human beings learning the way of love and justice, beyond the limits of cooperation and beyond the limits of kin and tribe and then of nation, as the only way in which persons in relation can flourish and be themselves with and from the difference of others.

The divine love by which the world and life on this planet is brought into being along so costly a path becomes incarnate, and is subject to the same costly path, and so the violent history of the world is visited on its Creator. Here God incarnate absorbs this visitation and suffers the cost of this long history of violence, initiated by creating and sustaining the world from the excess of divine love. Here God incarnate fully embodies the other way of 'making things make themselves', the way of love and justice. It turns out in fact that this love proves stronger than death. From within the world, the death and resurrection of God incarnate opens the world to the only future God

---

into why God creates by natural selection with all its apparent waste and suffering. I would link these strands in a doctrine of creation to the view that the incarnation is the inner meaning and purpose of creation and would have taken place without the occasion of a 'happy fault'. Implications for the doctrine of divine action in the world will have to be taken up another time, but will still be on the side of Moore's opposition to deism and pantheism. See also WC Platcher, *The Domestication of Transcendence* (Louiville: Westminster John Knox Press, 1996), 115, n. 12, where I first came across two of these three references to Aquinas.

desires for all things—risen from death and decay and sharing in the divine life. Finally justice will be done to the love, which initiated the creation of the world and proved to be its most passionate servant because justice will be done for the world.

Nevertheless it is another orientation, with other possibilities for life, to which humankind attends and finds more persuasive. In any of its forms, this orientation of individual and social life has come to be established as if it had a life of its own, as encompassing 'fictions', more living us than being lived by us. These peculiarly human 'fictions' continue to filter and unfold God's evolutionary way of 'making things make themselves', while still giving a place to God or the gods, even a place for love and justice, at least for one's own.

This path was given new scope and direction by the revolutionary changes in Europe in the sixteenth and seventeenth centuries. Hooker's model spells out the dynamics of this powerful process expanding in our own days to globalised social Darwinism, an 'imperial fiction', whose 'logic' is to be what in political discourse is called 'sovereign power': that power of which there is none greater. This is an encompassing surrogate of true life, a virulent life form that includes reducing human value to instrumental values, with personae serving desired ends, where the economy of desire is shaped by commodity production and market exchange, themselves more deeply driven and fed by attachment and reaction to the perceived underlying lack of intrinsic value and meaning to life.

Dissonance and resonance: Christ and the church

In the light of this good news, the church celebrates and announces to all the eternal purpose of God the Creator, to unite all things in heaven and earth in Christ the incarnate Word, through whom all things were created. The church is the community brought into being to witness to this God who invites humankind into the divine life, only lately opened in all its depths through Christ. To be and do this well the church has to attend to the *resonance* and the *dissonance* between Christ and the world.

In the gospel of Christ, the power of this future, intended in love from the beginning for all created things, even now reaches into our present, repeating anew in our lives the same *dissonance* and *resonance* as shook people when Jesus first proclaimed the good news of the reign of God. Amidst this shaking, the church is brought to birth by the word and the Spirit, as the community that is to be a sign of the times, where all people may find a saving foretaste of the powers of the age to come, both in word and sacrament, in the vitality of the community, in its charismata, in its bearing each other's burdens, in its faith, demonstrated by the 'foolish' courage of people's lives.

Being born and formed by this *dissonance* and *resonance*, the church is thereby called and sent into the same conflict and should expect to share the way of Jesus. This will include confronting the powerful 'fictions' of the times; standing with and for those set aside, disadvantaged and abused by these powerful 'fictions', those that are the least of Jesus' brothers and sisters; enjoying the glorious liberty of the children of God as we explore the 'original blessing' flourishing now in the power of the gospel, being more and more freed from the personal and structural distortions of sin, and imbued with a foretaste of the consummation planned and promised by God in Christ. We are all called to bear and explore this *dissonance* and *resonance*, to be a sign of the times, witnessing to the God who has the 'last word'.

All this assumes that the 'shaking' just mentioned does indeed form the church and issue in an authentic *resonance* between Christ and the church. We have to acknowledge that all this may be attenuated, resisted, neglected, forgotten, blocked, so that some churches find their relationship with Christ is marked by a particular *dissonance*, that ironically the church is indeed a sign of the times, even in its attempt to cover up its contradictions. This *dissonance* may be brought to light and felt a fresh by movements of the Word and the Spirit, whether in the church or the world. These movements again shake a church whose life, for example, resonates more with the remnants of an older established order, or the fashions of the latest one, rather than the *resonance* between the creation and the reign of God.[30]

The ambiguity of seductive fictions

But we should recognise that both the seduction of the world by its own encompassing 'fictions' and the worldly seduction of the church are manifestations of humankind's most 'original sin' and 'original blessing'. Just as the law is good and holy, yet can be used by the power of sin for other ends, so the 'original blessing' is good, yet can be used for other ends. The 'original blessing' continues amidst our

30. Revelation 2:1–3: 22, the seven letters to the seven churches, is a powerful example of the *dissonances* and *resonances* between Christ and the church.

following one or other persuasive possibilities for life apart from God, which in any form comes to have a life of its own, an encompassing fiction, structuring our lives, more living in us than lived by us. Yet, the 'original blessing' continues amidst the fact and fate of sin, never having been revoked by God.

The worldly 'fictions' present powerful and desirable surrogates of real life. This is because they are feeding off, manifesting and thereby unfolding, the 'original blessing', now filtered and distorted through these 'fictions'. Not withstanding this vast sinful structuring of life, there is still much that witnesses to the goodness, beauty and abundant creativity of God, even in the midst of and in some ways even by means of the misuse of the awesome dominion given to humankind. This 'double entendre' however, must be carefully disambiguated.

The people of any church are not isolated from the powerful and seductive surrogates of real life offered by the worldly 'fictions'. Hence the risk of being captivated and so captured by the encompassing worldly 'fictions' which are the false surrogates of true life, whether of the churches' own making, or of the culture in which it is immersed and which it imbibes. All the more reason for any church to know within its own life a more authentic *resonance* with the liberating power of the gospel of Jesus the Messiah. In this way the churches may come to 'see through' the encompassing worldly 'fictions' of the times, with all their seductive ambiguity, to better discern the good creation of God and use aright the 'original blessing' to serve the reign of God.

We can see that the church must position itself in society in ways that imitate and participate in the match and mismatch, the *dissonance* and the *resonance* between Christ and the world. But with the possibility of a *dissonance* or mismatch marking the relationship between Christ and the church, it is possible that any church may position itself or be positioned in a match/mismatch relationship to its society that is not on account of Christ. Were such a possibility realised in practice, it would eventually weaken the church's participation in the mission of Christ and the church's authority, which is authority for mission.

Based on my experience, I think the Anglican Church in Melbourne moved in that direction. Overall, we took for granted our success in the post-war boom. Since then the society has changed in ways that reduced our 'match' and increased our 'mismatch' to society. In the process we lost touch with most of three generations. Not just in the sense of numbers and age profile of those not involved in the church, but with their life-styles and cultures, with their different ways of being and relating as persons, with different spiritualities, sexualities and worldviews. These are the people whose lives are powerfully formed by the 'revolutions' and the other changes noted above, as distinct from earlier generations whose lives were formed in a different social context.

Anglicans persisted for too long in uncritically living off the social capital of our inherited ways of being part of and deeply embedded in, the daily life of Australians, which was changing rapidly. And we have been too attached to, too enamoured of our inherited ways of being church. This narcissism led us to mistake historical precedent for theological norm. We were thereby poorly positioned to weigh deeply enough the changes going on, much less those needed. Nor, for these and other reasons such as our actual devaluing of theological reflection outside an academic setting, were we well placed to appropriate the tradition afresh and so to risk ourselves in exploring faithful and novel ways of engaging our changing social context. Our attachments to our inherited ways of being church meant that we found ourselves increasingly in a mismatched relation to our own culture, our own times, but, alas, I think not mainly on account of Christ.

In my experience of the Anglican Church in Melbourne, we have all found it a difficult struggle to take stock of how deeply attached we are to our inherited ways of being church, of how effectively we were positioned within the dominant modern culture, accommodating ourselves to serve the private spiritual needs of people living with the scientific, technological and social 'realities' carried by the dominant, secular, industrial society, including the types of 'personae' it required and engendered. We came to provide the 'icing on the cake' in regard to cultural, national and personal identities, which were daily being formed in an emerging social context pervaded by an increasingly turbulent change process that increased the *dissonances* and reduced the *resonances* between society and our inherited ways of being church.

There were people in the churches, including the Anglican church, who appreciated the signs of the times in the period after World War II, and there were and are many efforts to change, both denominational and ecumenical initiatives, and from the senior denominational leadership as well as local parishes, chaplaincies and church agencies. Among many continuing initiatives, Jubilee 2000 was the most noticeable on the world stage. Locally, communities exploring faithful and novel ways of engaging our changing social context do bear fruit. Not too far from now, these will be the only church communities in existence.

3.2 Conclusion

There are more empirical accounts of a healthy church, based on studying growing congregations. I regard them as valuable and make use of them in my work in Melbourne. However, I also need a more theological account of what counts as a healthy church and this is what I hope to have communicated in this vignette. The last section takes a few matters from sections 2 and 3 to briefly illustrate what they imply about becoming a healthy church in our social context.

4. Becoming a healthy church in our society

Along the lines expounded in the theological vignette, I take this to mean that Christian communities are becoming healthy parts of the one, holy, catholic and apostolic church, demonstrating their ecumenical desire for communion and their goodwill for all people in our society and inviting all the world to taste and see that God in Christ is good!

On the views presented above, the church is called and sent in the power of the Spirit to participate in Jesus' own mission, and so enter into vulnerable but victorious conflict with the powers of life, misoriented and established falsely as a life of its own. This requires the church to announce the good news of the reign of God revealed in Christ and hence to name and act on the *dissonances* and the *resonances* between Christ and the world. This calls for a more authentic *resonance* between Christ and the church and calls the church to be a more authentic servant of the true interests of the world.

A more authentic resonance between Christ and the church

I began the paper by outlining my image of the Anglican Church in Melbourne. I do not consider it to be in a healthy state. This thought is strengthened in the light of the theological reflection on what counts as a healthy church.

That reflection may be summarised as follows. The marks of apostolicity, catholicity and holiness of the church show us the length, breadth, height and depth of our mission to engage the world on account of Christ. The unity of the church in Christ is the way we together, have access to the 'fullness' of Christ, that good life which

Christ gives now and therewith all that is needed for the mission of such proportions.

Our overall lack of health in measured by the lack of these proportions in our mission and the extent to which we have adjusted to the lack. In these circumstances it is as if we do not need access to the 'fullness' of Christ. Why would we not need access to the 'fullness' of Christ? This is to ask about that 'other law' at work in us.

It could be due to our believing that access to the 'fullness' of Christ is more individualised than Scripture teaches, more a matter for this person, this community, as if our being members one of another in practice were not crucial to all enjoying this access. It could be due to a want of confidence in Christ and his power to transform our lives and the lives of others. It could be due to our not wanting such transformation because our loyalties and affections are otherwise attached to something of secondary importance, mistakenly treated as of first importance, and therefore more manageable by us just as we are.

Let us consider two examples to do with mission that call for a more authentic *resonance* between Christ and the church, in this case the Anglican church.

The church is catholic

Under the mark of catholicity I argued that the fulfilling of the great commission requires us to radically multiply the number and diversify the forms of Christian communities. The diversity means that there will be very large mega churches, solid traditional parishes, both large and small, and a myriad of other communities, where the emphasis will be on 'traveling light'.

This radical multiplying and diversifying, calls for all of the marks of our being in Christ to be realised, but let me focus on the first mark of the church. This is our unity in Christ, which here means such a community of communities, such eccentricity, such creativity, such esteem of one another, such a multiplicity of gifts of the Spirit, such a play of form and freedom in Christ, such engagement with each other and therefore such conflicts, such a disclosure of the betrayer at hand within each of us and each community, but now owned and not on the loose, that there is such access to the 'fullness' of Christ for communities old and new, large and small, that we be overwhelmed by the divine life coursing through us, our distortions, our sin not withstanding, but rather all being purged in the energies of a still greater goodness, who calls us on. Such a prospect seems to me to essential to the church being truly catholic, fulfilling the great evangelical commission.

It is no surprise that such a view might evoke a litany of obstacles. The issue is whether there will be a robust conversation about our life as a church or whether it will be prematurely limited in order to avoid facing the obstacles. The latter path leads to compliance not commitment. The alternative is to get robust agreement on the implications of the great commission and see what we need in order to pursue it. Together we would then have need of access to the 'fullness' of Christ, whom we trust to call forth presently hidden or withheld resources. This last, because for want of a more excellent way, people go their own way, placing their resources in the service of an inspiring and authentic vision. The challenge for leadership to initiate, maintain and protect this conversation and ensure that it is acted on, using well the resources that become available as a result.

To pursue this mark of catholicity as a sign of a healthy church would also call for local Anglican churches to take hold of the task, not just of handing on their living church community for the future, but also replicating a Christian community for others who are not engaged by their local church. This in turn requires many more people of the church to have moved from 'belonging' faith to 'owned' faith[31] and be willing and able to join in the founding of a new Christian community, which may be very different from the one that has sustained them.

Enough has been said to indicate how easy it would be to feel inadequate to the task. To pursue this mark of catholicity as a sign of being a healthy church would call for a power beyond what we have access to at the moment, and a power of which we were confident, and that power is Christ. To pursue the great commission in this way would call for a renewal of our commitment to Christ, and to one another, so that our way of being church is more aligned with rather than against the grain of our being in Christ.

---

31. This recalls the well known work of John Westerhoff. I thank the Rev Dr Paul Dalzell for many discussions on this theme. Of particular interest his thesis for Doctor of Ministry Studies, *Two Paths One Process?: Exploring the Lived Experience of Participants in Two Forms of Evangelism in Two Anglican Churches in Brisbane* (Melbourne College of Divinity, 2003). Dalzell explores and compares the process of a group involved in ALPHA and a group undertaking the Catechumenate. Westerhoff said this was the best thesis he had read in forty years.

The church is holy—But we become like what we worship!

To introduce another example, I recall a connection between worship and mission and the ordained ministry of oversight of the church, which for Anglicans means the bishops and priests, who preside at the liturgy, who teach and preach, and who are to lead a missionary church.

In worship we celebrate the great divine economy for the whole creation lately revealed in Christ. In mission we enter into the working out of that divine economy in our time and place. According to the Bible we become like what we worship.[32] The result of worshipping 'idols' is the despoiling, diminishing of human wellbeing: we have eyes and cannot see, mouths and cannot speak, etc. This is the cost of submitting to the 'realities' of the encompassing 'fictions' discussed above and acquiring the personae they require. By contrast the worship of the living God, whose first command authorises and calls forth all our heart, mind, soul and strength, who is therefore life giving for us, both individually and collectively.

It is hardly a surprising suggestion that the people of the church, including the clergy, might carry into worship quite a range of understandings and symbols of themselves, of life and of God. That there might be some want of 'orthodoxy' in all of this is also hardly surprising. Indeed it ought to be the stuff of an energising, ongoing 'conversation' within the church. Can that conversation be found in our midst? My remarks about what it means for the church to be holy is one contribution to that conversation.

Of course, there may be nothing to 'worry' about in any of this. But how shall we tell? If it is true that we become like what we worship, we can gain some hint of what we worship, by reflecting on what we have become. Where we are weak in mission it is a serious question as to whether our worship and ourselves as worshippers are carriers of tacit understandings and symbols of ourselves, of life and of God, that seriously misinform our worship of the holy God, and of our living. We need to take stock of the 'culture', in church and society, as the bearer of a more powerful 'cult' compared to our worship.

There is an inescapable connection between worship and mission. Where one is strong or weak so is the other. Either way leadership needs to be as innocent as a dove and wise a serpent in recognising

---

32. Psalm 115, 135, and even more, Jeremiah 2:4.

where that 'other law' in the form of the more powerful 'cult' is at work in our corporate life, and lead the church to worship the living God rather than a surrogate. The risk is that our worship provides the 'icing on the cake' of our identities, daily informed by the social realities of our high-tech society that are able to reach into our lives and form us as persons.

Hopefully, this daily formation would be disrupted through our worship exposing us to the narrative and other effective symbols of the reign of God revealed in Christ and by a daily practice of following Christ. Besides producing this *dissonance* I suggest there is a *resonance* between this exposure and daily following of Christ and the ab-original gift and impulse of life from God, by which we are continually sustained in existence. This *resonance* calls forth this gift of life within us, opening our lives to the life of the triune God, for which we are created. We are no longer bound by, even as we bear the marks of, all the formation of ourselves as persons to which we are subject. The combination of this *dissonance* and *resonance* makes it possible for individuals and worshipping communities to 'see through' the formative powers of the world in which we live. Then we enter more fully into the mission of Christ in and for the world.

Theologically, this is a reasonable hope, but is what we have become due to a lack of the word being preached and the sacraments administered? I think not. St. John said plainly that we cannot claim to love the God we cannot see if we cannot love those we do see.[33] I take that to apply across the board: worship and mission and the fellowship that it needs and expresses are intimately connected. Where one is weak so is the other and perhaps like a certain young man, we only come to our senses about our fellowship, our worship and our mission, when our situation becomes desperate.[34]

The church as servant of the true interests of the world

The true interests of the world and of the church are to know the reality of the reign of God revealed in Christ, now in anticipation, finally in glory. This is a contentious claim.

Almost certainly it will seem either unintelligible or incredible to most people not Christians. For Christians it could be far from obvious. Perhaps some other account of God or God in Christ defines

33. 1 John 4:20.

34. Cf Luke 15: 11–32.

the world's true interest. Other Christians could also find it far from obvious because for them only what the world testifies about its own interests should be heeded, while for still other Christians it is so obvious there is no need to listen to what the world thinks is its true interest.

My position is that the church should bear witness to the kind of world it is, both in terms that the world testifies to itself and in terms of the kind of God revealed in Christ. Given that the church may be in a mismatched relation to Christ, it is possible that in some circumstances the world's testimony to itself may be one way the Spirit speaks to the churches. Either way it is important to listen to what the world says about itself.

This servant role is possible for any church only to the extent that it submits to a more authentic *resonance* with the life of Christ and invites everyone into the knowledge of Christ. Thus the previous section highlights the first and most important way the church is to be a servant of the true interests of the world.

In this servant role the church names and acts on the *dissonances* and *resonances* between the realities of the reign of God revealed in Christ and the realities of the society in which the church is called to live. This takes place at the 'in your face' level of daily life and at the 'covert' level of social change.

At the 'in your face' level of daily life

Suppose the churches publicly 'named' where and in what way the values, ideas, movements, inventions, changes, energies, creativity evident in our society *resonate* with ways of God revealed in Christ. This would be to acknowledge the intimations of God's presence in people's lives and the unfolding of the 'original blessing', while allowing for, but in due course naming the distortions of that blessing.

This 'naming' would surely introduce a very positive stance into the way the church positions itself in relation to society on account of Christ. It would surely promote a many sided conversation and cooperation between churches and the wider community, whether with people from other religious traditions or from none.

This positive stance would be a significant change for many in the churches and may lead to a change in the way many people with no religious tradition automatically position themselves in relation to the church and its gospel.

It may be felt there is a risk for the church in 'naming' these *resonances*, as if there would then no need to speak of Christ. It is clear that the people on the right hand of the Judge in Matthew 25 had no theological idea of what they had been doing in serving others, rather were they doing this as if God were not a consideration. We should not be concerned that the people in whose lives we find these *resonances* do not understand themselves in anything like these terms. Who knows what may follow from conversations about the 'unknown God', everywhere at work, even now the secret of their lives, but a secret openly displayed in Christ. The church should certainly not think that this naming obviates the need to meet people with the good news of Christ, nor accept that view if it is expressed by people in whose lives these *resonances* are recognized and 'named'.

The 'revolutions' mentioned earlier are ambiguous, with both *dissonances* and *resonances* between these revolutions and the God revealed in Christ. They are part and parcel of daily life for us all. Yet they are not the focus of attention and reflection in many Anglican communities. There is a need for a developing grass-roots reflection in Anglican communities on how we in fact live and how we might better live under these contemporary conditions and so appreciate the *resonances*, contest the *dissonances* and resist their being taken-or-granted.

It could be though that the *dissonances* were easier to 'name'. On one level such *dissonances* would include the unfinished work of reconciliation between Indigenous and other Australians; the dreadful state of the land on which we live; the treatment of refugees coming to Australia; the continuing level of unemployment well above the official estimate; the number of children in families living in poverty and the abuse of children; whether sexually or other ways; the cynicism about all forms of institutional life, political, religion, the law and law enforcement and business; the increased insecurity and fear about the way life is going.

The churches and other organisations and individuals have been and are involved in not only naming, but working to do something about these and other *dissonances* between the way life is going in our society and the God revealed in Christ. In the case of the sexual abuse of children and women, the church has been part of the *dissonance*, which includes the denial of justice to victims and the cover-up to protect the institution.

In the light of the discussions on attending to our social context and the theological vignette, these and many other matters are indeed where the churches should be focused. And this in fact is where the welfare agencies of the churches as well as many local Christian communities are already focused.

But there is more to consider for these matters are very much if not entirely at the 'in your face' level of the way life is going.

At the covert level of social change

I have argued that this turbulent social change is driven by a vast 'societal change engine' operating at the conjunction of scientific inquiry, the generation of new technologies, commodity production and market exchange. So comprehensive is this turbulent social change that it has come to be treated as 'natural'. This is so obvious that it barely draws attention to how deeply insinuated is this attitude to our lives. This 'naturalising' of the change process is one expression of the naturalistic worldview that over the last four hundred years has become a widely absorbed grounding assumptions about the kind of world in which we live.

This naturalistic worldview is daily engrained in us by the 'in your face level' of the way life is going which has insinuated within it the sense that such change is 'natural'. I have sought to understand this encompassing turbulent change and its being 'naturalised' in terms as a virulent life form, a globalising, social Darwinism, an 'imperial fiction' because its 'logic' includes becoming what in political theory is called 'sovereign power': that power of which there is none greater.

This 'fiction' or better this 'lie' presents a powerful and desirable surrogate of real life. This is because it is feeding off, manifesting and thereby unfolding, the 'original blessing', now filtered through the 'fictions'. But this is not the only source of its power. This encompassing 'lie' functions as a surrogate 'divinity' by which meaning and value for life—human and otherwise—is reduced to what is of instrumental values for this 'divinity'. Thus another source of its power is that does something like a 'god job', which is needed when other 'gods' are either banished or merely given a place on the 'icing' of the cultural cake.

Finally this same covert level of the encompassing 'fictions' evokes a still stronger attachment to and dependence on the overt accelerating, turbulent economy of change. This is done by showing that those who do not fit in and adapt to this way of structuring life are left behind as 'debris' in the wake of change. More deeply, people imbibe the insinuation that there is no underlying intrinsic value and meaning to life and the undermining of alternative sources of value and meaning.

The point is that the older fabric of life once woven through more frequent and more settled face to face engagements with others, is now unravelling to the point of losing the capacity to ground a felt sense of value unconditioned. This form of life is rendered 'retro', being reframed and threaded by more technologically extended abstract forms of communication, based on the 'real absence' rather than the 'real presence' of those communicating. These more abstract forms of communication include the media saturation of daily life, which mediates the conditions for acquiring value. Individuals are then more and more vulnerable to being drawn into forming 'selves' or 'personae' serving desired ends, within an economy of desire shaped by commodity production and market exchange that testifies to itself as having 'no limits'. [35]

There is surely a *dissonance* between the reality of the reign of God revealed in Christ, the true sovereign power, and this vast 'societal change engine'. It is one thing to (begin) to name the *dissonances*, it is another thing to act on it. What action is called for and what is possible? Surely the action called for is to change the 'change engine'. Many may think this proposal is monumentally mad, well beyond any talk of 'David and Goliath'. I can imagine people arguing that it has nothing to do with becoming a healthy church.

Instead I hear its *resonance* with the 'foolishness' of 1 Corinthians 1: 25 and the impact of 'leaven' on the whole loaf.[36] Given the theological and social analysis, then it is indeed part of being a healthy church. But furthermore, this is hardly a new thought. Jubilee 2000 was a world-wide movement to cancel unpayable, crushing debt of many third world nations. Many people are critical of various aspects of the global 'change engine', but especially the way many nations have been

35. This point touches on a number of themes that are a part of a much larger theoretical position developed at *Arena*, both in the journal and magazine. I am much indebted to the work of Geoff Sharp and John Hinkson and many others at *Arena*, including Simon Cooper. A good introduction to the larger theoretical position is in G Sharp, J Hinkson, and S Cooper, *Scholars and Entrepreneurs: Universities in Crisis* (North Carlton: *Arena* Publications, 2002).

36. Luke 13: 20–21.

excluded from sharing in its benefits. The economist Joseph Stiglitz[37] is one of them. Many nations, including Australia, call for the removal of farm subsidies in the EU and the USA which have dreadful impact on poor nations. On the theological and social analysis presented above all these are examples of the distortion of the 'original blessing' whereby all men and women have 'dominion' over the earth in order that they may be fruitful and multiply. The distortion is part of a globalised social Darwinism. Just as there is a profound *resonance* between creation and the reign of God revealed in Christ, there can be no question of ignoring the *dissonance* between the reign of God and the global 'change engine'.

In what ways could the churches, hope to have any impact on the vast, global 'change engine'? This is a question for another occasion. In concluding this paper I want to highlight three of the many things the Anglican church in Melbourne could do: contesting the naturalistic worldview; helping promote another way of organising work and developing a spirituality for daily life—confronting the 'powers and principalities'.

Contesting a naturalistic worldview

This naturalism draws on a philosophical appropriation of the natural sciences, which adds, 'and all there is what the natural sciences say there is or is complex configurations of what the natural sciences say there is'. Not to contest the matter is to surrender the natural sciences to being so appropriated within this naturalism and by various cultural processes (education, work, media) become widely taken-for-granted.

There are rationally available grounds for contesting this naturalistic worldview and for seeking a richer worldview than naturalism.[38] The things for which natural sciences cannot (not, *has not*) provide an adequate account are the grounds for seeking a richer worldview than naturalism; for example, human inquiry conducted in the natural and formal sciences and everyday life, consciousness and

---

37. J Stilitz, *GLOBALISATION and its Discontents* (Penguin, 2002)

38. WL Craig, and JP Moreland, editors, *Naturalism: A Critical Analysis* (London: Routledge, 2000); DR Griffin, *Religion and Scientific Naturalism: Overcoming the Conflicts* (Albany: State University of New York Press, 2000); *Naturalism defeated?: Essays on Plantinga's Evolutionary Argument Against Naturalism*, edited by J Beilby (Ithaca: Cornell University Press, 2002).

intentionality. Critically building on the work of Professor Roy Frieden,[39] my doctoral work has been developing the explanation and derivation of the laws of fundamental physics in terms of Fisher information. On this approach to physics the physical universe has just those physical laws and space-time structure you would expect as *a logical consequence* of the assumption that empirical inquiry is conductable anywhere in the universe, along with some other physical knowledge, which does not entail these laws. This result cannot be explained either in terms of full on naturalism (physicalism), or evolutionary theory or 'multiple universes'. On the other hand this result invites an explanation in terms of the universe being designed for some purpose that includes the universe being knowable by empirical inquiry. There are various possible contenders for the 'designer' but, any contender must have the characteristics of some kind of agency that is the natural ground of the rational agency that shows up in inquiries in the natural sciences and in every day life.[40]

The church has many people with resources to engage in the task of rationally contesting naturalism and formulating a richer worldview. I think there is great interest among people, young people especially, on the question of what kind of world it is in which we live. It would be quite possible to develop educational programmes that are engaging and accessible for a wide range of people. The churches have many relevant resources for doing this. This is a task that has been attempted many times and is still needed after four hundred years. We may reverse Steven Weinberg's statement: the more we understand the world the more we grasp its intrinsic purpose.

For an entirely distinct approach we can point to efforts to formulate a theology of nature rather than a natural theology. In its various forms this work aims to produce a theological worldview that holds together the scientific, technological and social dimensions of our

---

39. RB Frieden, *Physics from Fisher Information: A Unification*, (Cambridge: Cambridge University Press, 1989). My work has been conducted within the Department of History and Philosophy of Science at the University of Melbourne.
40. I am interested in making an argument for a natural theology. Here I am much helped, for example by WL Craig and JP Moreland, editors, (2000), *op cit*, *Philosophical Foundations for a Christian Worldview* (Downers Grove: InterVarsity Press, 2003).

life in a different configuration from naturalism.[41] This opens up the work relating cosmology and theology, to cosmology and Christology, and cosmology and eschatology. We can also point to critiques of our culture and of Christianity's submission to modernity.[42]

These ways of naming and contesting the naturalistic worldview needs to be done in intellectual and popular idioms, so that the widest range of people can be engaged with the aim of it becoming the way people make sense of the world, at once strong enough to inform daily living, and robust enough to keep developing.

Another way of working

The question is how could the churches hope to have any impact on the vast, global 'change engine'? Another response to this question concerns the possibility of how we organize work and to what end, and how work daily engrains a naturalised worldview without ever mentioning the term. Would that the values of an alternative theological worldview might be engrained by daily work. Here I think the cooperativist traditions offer a resource.[43] It would need people with the relevant knowledge, commitments and skill, to form working cooperatives that would be driven by a worldview and values very different from the market-place, but would be able to survive and thrive in the market-place. The different values would include a different relation between those who owned and those who worked the business, for they would be the same; a better relation between work and family; and work and the environment.

---

41. See the five volume work in science and theology pursued jointly by the Vatican Observatory and the Centre for Theology and Natural Sciences, edited by R Russell, *et al,* examining scientific perspectives on divine action..
42. I have found particularly helpful *Radical Orthodoxy: A New Theology*, edited by J Milbank, C Pickstock and G Ward (London, Routledge, 1999); J Milbank, *The Word Made Strange: Theology, Language, Culture* (Cambridge, Mass: Blackwell Publishers, 1997), and *Theology and Social Theory: Beyond Secular Reason* (Oxford: Blackwell, 1993); and C Gunton, *The Triune Creator: A Historical and Systematic Study*, (Grand Rapids: Eerdmanns, 1998).
43. Race Matthews, *Jobs of Their Own* (Sydney: Pluto Press, 1999). From a very different tradition, but with examples of Christians taking initiatives of the kind here envisaged, see, David Oliver and James Thwaites, *Church That Works* (Word Publishing, 2001).

The aim would be to achieve a very sustainable business and a very much better form of life, both embodying the core features of another view of the world, briefly indicated above. I think if this were achievable, more and more people would be attracted to this way of organising and developing work. Here the 'original blessing' with its real powers would be able to live and work more and more freed from the distortions manifested in the turbulent, globalised social Darwinism. Then there could develop a real engagement of the wider society on the differences between this form of life and work and the 'change engine' driving social change at present.

One opportunity in Melbourne might be a flow on from the fairware campaign by churches, trade unions and other community groups in support of sweatshop workers. At a Melbourne fashion show last year the Brotherhood of St Laurence's new low cost design 'Hunters & Gatherers' label was the only contributor that had signed up to the fair ware agreement not to use sweatshop labour. The message was not lost on other fashion labels. The question is what would it take for the men, women and children who are caught up in 'sweat shop' labour for the rag trade, to form themselves into a cooperative and hopefully go from strength to strength?[44] Is it possible to find within and beyond the churches people who could work together to support the development of more cooperatives? I think even one stunning working example of a cooperative that did indeed embody a different way of life, daily reinforcing a different worldview in the participants, would be a powerful stimulus for attracting such supporters for change in the direction I envisage: change the 'change engine'.

'Powers and principalities'—a spirituality of everyday life

I spoke earlier of Jesus facing and breaking all the *powers* of life misoriented and established falsely as a life of its own and that we are called into the same conflict. I also spoke of some of the encompassing 'fictions' of our day, and their power to structure our lives including our sense of 'self'.

To engage these encompassing 'fictions' we have to be able to 'see through' the realities that are taken-for-granted. This 'seeing through' occurs where the power and authority of the encompassing 'fictions' is

44. I am indebted to Fr Robert Holland of the Brotherhood of St Laurence for this question and the answer to which he is party.

broken by a still stronger power and our eyes opened to the reality on which the 'fictions' are parasitic, which they distort and hide.

A stronger power is at work for people's eyes are opened because God is at work in and for the world, both incognito as the power of the demand and desire for truth and justice, and openly in the power of the gospel of Christ. The power of the gospel recapitulates and carries further our 'seeing through the fictions' and apprehending the reality, which they distort and hide. The capacity for such 'seeing through' is no cheap grace nor is the work of resisting and engaging these powers. This spirituality of daily life of naming, resisting and challenging the powers and principalities of the encompassing 'imperial fiction' can be greatly enhanced by forms of spiritual companionship and guidance. The church has resources here, which could be and are made available not only to Christians but to people who cannot yet receive the gospel, but, like the scribe, 'are not far from the kingdom'.

Conclusion

I began this paper by asking how we should understand the *dissonances* and *resonances* between the church and society. The part of the church that I know best is the Anglican Church in Melbourne. My image of this church is that overall it is far from healthy. Hence the need to consider what counts as a healthy church and what relationship should there be between a healthy church and our society. Inevitably this requires some understanding of our society. This starting point opened a rich field of inquiry into the many dimensions in the theme of '*dissonances* and *resonances*'. The proposed answer to the opening question is to understand the *dissonances* and *resonances* between church and society in the light of the *dissonances* and *resonances* between Christ and the world.

Contributors

Tony Abbott is a member of the Liberal Party of Australia, elected Federal Member for Warringah, New South Wales in 1994. At the time of giving the paper in this volume he was Minister for Employment. At the time of printing he is Minister for Health.

Chris Evans is a member of the Australian Labor Party, elected Senator for Western Australia in 1993. At the time of giving the paper in this volume he was Shadow Minister for Family Services and the Aged with responsibility for Aged Care, childcare and disability services. At the time of printing he is Shadow Minister for Defence.

Alexander Downer is a member of the Liberal Party of Australia, elected Federal Member for Mayo in 1984. At the time of printing he is Minister for Foreign Affairs.

Ronald Wilson is former President of the National Assembly of the Uniting Church in Australia, former President of the National Human Rights and equal Opportunity Commission; Co-Chair of the National Enquiry into the Separation of Aboriginal and Torres Strait Islander Children from their Families and a retired Judge of the High Court of Australia.

William Deane is former Governor-General of the Commonwealth of Australia and a retired Judge of the High Court of Australia.

Brian Howe is a Uniting Church Minister, Professorial Associate in the Centre for Public Policy, University of Melbourne, a lecturer in Faith and Society at the United Faculty of Theology, Melbourne and former Deputy Prime Minister of Australia.

James Haire is a former President of the Uniting Church in Australia and held this position when he gave this paper in 2001. At time of printing he is Director of the Australian Centre for Christianity and Culture in Canberra.

Allan Patience is Professor of Politics in the University of Papua New Guinea, and Sometime Professor of Political Science at Victoria University, Melbourne.

Linda Campbell is Senior Lecturer in Social Work at the University of Melbourne.

Joe Caddy is Director of Catholic Social Services in Melbourne.

Hilary Berthon is a Policy Adviser with Uniting*Care* Australia in Canberra.

Lin Hattfield-Dodds is National Director of Uniting*Care* Australia in Canberrra.

Ray Cleary is Executive Director of Anglicare Victoria, a Canon of St Paul's Anglican Cathedral Melbourne, and Chair of Anglican Social Responsibility Commission, Melbourne.

John Pettman is a Uniting Church Minister. At the time of giving this paper he was Chairman of Uniting*Care* Australia. He is now retired and lives in Tasmania.

Geoff Schirmer is a Lutheran Pastor. At the time of giving this paper he was Lutheran Chaplain to hospitals in Melbourne. He is now retired and lives in Melbourne.

Harry Herbert is Executive Director for Uniting*Care* in New South Wales and the Australian Capital Territory in Sydney.

Stephen Ames is a Canon of St Paul's Anglican Cathedral, Melbourne, and Lecturer in the Department of History and Philosophy of Science at the University of Melbourne.

Francis Sullivan is Executive Director of Catholic Health Australia in Canberra.

Sue Leppert is Executive Director of Anglicare for Canberra and Goulburn.

Author Index

Subject Index